YOUNG MEN IN PRISON

YOUNG MEN IN PRISON
The criminal identity explored
through the rules of behaviour

Michael Little

Dartington Social Research Unit

Dartmouth

R42

Published by
Dartmouth Publishing Company Limited
Gower House, Croft Road, Aldershot,
Hants. GU11 3HR, England

and

Gower Publishing Company,
Old Post Road, Brookfield, Vermont 05036
USA

British Library Cataloguing in Publication Data
Little, Michael, 1958-
    Young men in prison: the criminal identity explored
    through the rules of behaviour
    1. Great Britain. Young offenders
    I. Title

ISBN 1 85521 093 2

Printed in Great Britain by
Billing & Sons Ltd, Worcester

Contents

List of tables

Acknowledgements

Many people have supported me in my research for this book. Colleagues at the City of Birmingham Polytechnic, particularly Jane Calvert and Ron Vannelli, helped me fashion and develop ideas on which the study is based and this report could not have been completed satisfactorily without their support. The work builds upon methods used by Peter Marsh at the University of Oxford and I am indebted to him for his tutelage and guidance. Mike Smith at the University of Bath kindly advised me throughout this project, patiently commenting on each stage of the book as it was produced. Norman Tutt, Director of Social Services in Leeds, has written a preface to the book, placing it in the wider social and historical context of services for delinquent children.

Whilst writing this book, I have worked at the Dartington Social Research Unit, a Department of Health designated Unit, part of the University of Bristol. Colleagues at Dartington have advised and guided me with great patience and good humour and, in the process, I have learned more about research and writing reports than I dare to admit. So thanks to Margot Blake, Brenda Bullock, Roger Bullock, Hedy Cleaver, Debbie Doyle, Ken Hosie, Michael Kelly, Spencer Millham and Angela Williams at Dartington.

This research was not funded, it was completed independently in my own time, but Elmgrant Trust have kindly contributed to the cost of this book.

Finally, without the assistance of the Home Office and the governors, prison officers and administrative staff in the two participating penal institutions this research could not have been undertaken. The parents of the prisoners gave me permission to interview their children and, of course, none of the following pages would be possible without the help of the young men who talked with great intimacy about their lives. Needless to say, for reasons of confidentiality, none of their names can be given.

I am deeply grateful to them all.

Preface

In the United Kingdom we lock up more young people than any other country in Western Europe. Despite a large number of initiatives for young teenage delinquents, relatively little has been developed for those adolescents who persistently offend, particularly those who commit domestic burglaries. For this group policies are retributive, degrading and unimaginative; they are also inefficient. Three-quarters of youth custody graduates reoffend within two years of leaving, contradicting the views of those who believe that reform and deterrence spring from humiliation, punishment and squalor.

Young Men in Prison explains why these views are false and based on wrong assumptions about human behaviour. Michael Little demonstrates that long custodial experiences fuel the criminal identity of young offenders and make further crime a viable course for survival. He explains how this occurs and demonstrates the social psychology theory which makes this sequence of events predictable.

The study focuses on young peoples' views of themselves and the ways these are shaped by the formal and informal rules of prison life. The author divides the criminal experiences into discrete episodes - the first serious offence, life on the margins of prison, the initial prison experience and the point at which restriction of liberty becomes part of an accepted life style.

By looking at different types of rules at each stage - general rules of society, the formal rules of prison, rules guiding the interaction and beliefs of prisoners - clear changes in the motivations and perceptions of inmates can be shown over time.

The end product of our interventions is a disaster. Rather than the reformed delinquent striving to make good, the system produces bitter, angry and lonely young men living in a fantasy world. Further offending resolves these difficulties, hence the familiar rake's progress of crimes, custody, anomie and isolation.

I whole-heartedly recommend this well-researched and balanced discussion of a serious social problem, more especially since through meticulous research it demonstrates what many of us have known and declared, namely that young offenders' institutions are Universities of Crime rather the Universities of Reform. Michael Little has demonstrated how this phenomenon occurs and supports our rhetoric with clear evidence. It saddens me that despite advances in medical science and improvements in services for handicapped and disabled people, our approaches to persistent offenders remains archaic and little influenced by research. Our approaches are still rooted in the 18th Century and the cells in which some of our young people are currently incarcerated were not only built at that time but have also remained unchanged, as has the basis of their use. This book offers us new information we cannot ignore if we wish to make our interventions with young offenders worthy of a wealthy country with a proud tradition of welfare and humanity.

Professor Norman Tutt

1. Introduction

This is a book about the criminal identity of young property offenders whose crimes, such as burglary and car-theft, have resulted in their being remanded in a penal establishment or sentenced to a period of youth custody. It is a study based on interviews with forty-five young people who were asked to look back on their lives and explain the pattern of events which led to their being incarcerated. Such a strategy is not, in itself, novel but this investigation seeks to break new ground by applying a method previously untried by researchers interested in young offenders. In this book, the young offender's criminal identity is seen to develop during a *career* consisting of a series of *episodes*. What the young offender does in each of these episodes is largely guided by *rules of behaviour* and, by identifying and understanding these rules, a picture of the criminal identity is assembled.

The behaviour of the young people under scrutiny enjoins considerable resource, brings misery to many and adversely affects the quality of millions of lives. They break into, steal from and damage people's homes and take joy rides in cars. They can be blamed for the anxiety about empty houses and parked cars displayed by those who have yet to become victims. They are partly responsible for the increased surveillance in department stores, for increased insurance premiums and prices of goods. They keep many professional people fully occupied; social workers, police, probation and police officers are amongst those who seek to divert, deter and contain young offenders. Moreover, the subjects of this study endure the most uncomfortable of circumstances as a result of their crimes. Lastly, but not least, they embarrass and worry members of their own family. Why do they do it?

There have, of course, been many explanations for juvenile crime, most of which are plausible and helpful in understanding aspects of the problem. There are those who view delinquency as a primitive urge, a natural response amongst groups whose particular physiological or genetic make-up leads them to be criminal. Others view delinquency as a social problem resulting from, for example, individuals' inability to achieve desired goals legitimately. Recently, criminologists have focused upon the choices offenders make when deciding to break the law, working on the premise that the car thief will only steal a car if it is in his best interests to do so.

This book does not attempt to disprove or champion any of these or other explanations. Although those who focus on the interaction between groups of offenders and view crime as the outcome of an offender's choices or decisions have been the most helpful in shaping this study, the works of a number of writers have been useful. However, this book does attempt to look at offenders' interactions and choices in a new way by applying a method of investigation which will identify the rules of behaviour used by the young people under scrutiny. What are these rules of behaviour?

Episodes and rules

Many social scientists have sought to identify the principles which underpin everyday life but none has been very successful in developing a method which can be applied to the behaviour of different groups of people. The psychologist Rom Harré, however, has devised an approach which has formed the basis of studies into, for example, borstal girls, New York gangs, football hooligans and school-children in the classroom. In a series of books and articles, Harré has forwarded a theoretical perspective and method which challenge traditional sociological and psychological approaches to social behaviour, preferring techniques which seek deeper understanding of human action.

Harré proposes that social life is best understood when divided into its component episodes. Episodes are defined as 'any sequence of happenings in which human beings engage which has some principle of unity'. A distinction is then made between formal and informal episodes. Formal episodes are said to be determined by the participants following explicit rules which can be publicly stated. The laws of the state and rules of a game could both be cited as examples of rules which guide behaviour in formal episodes. Informal episodes also have rules which act as a guide to behaviour, but these are usually covert. Indeed, although those taking part in the event will be aware of the rules they are following, they are seldom able to articulate them and, consequently, researchers find them difficult to identify.

The value and significance of understanding social events and behaviour in this way is that the method can be used as a way of analysing systematically individuals' accounts of their behaviour. The suggestion is that, as with formal episodes, informal episodes can be understood by comprehending the rules of behaviour. Rules are defined as 'propositions which guide social action through the actor being aware of the rules and their prescriptions'. As with rules in formal episodes, such as the laws of the state, individuals can break a rule but, when it is broken, it is difficult for researchers to know why.

Nonetheless, by focusing upon rules it will be possible to achieve a better understanding of the perspectives of the young people interviewed in prison and, in particular, to comprehend their motivation and rationale in pursuing a criminal career.

Many of these definitions and terms may evoke feelings of *déjà vu* amongst readers familiar with the terminology of the social sciences. Is there any similarity between 'formal' and 'enigmatic' episodes on the one hand and the 'formal' and 'informal' social systems scrutinised by sociologists on the other? Perhaps a 'rule' differs little from a 'social norm', another tool of analysis successfully used by sociologists and anthropologists. There are, indeed, many areas of overlap and these are carefully considered later in the study.

Episode analysis has a clear attraction for the study of delinquency. Young people's offending can be a puzzling, almost mysterious activity, particularly when viewed from the perspective of the instigator. However, before this approach could be used in this study, it was necessary to clarify, adapt and develop some of the propositions. To begin with, the parameters of a delinquent episode were not clear. The unpredictable nature of young offenders' crimes made it difficult to identify when one event finished and another started. Secondly, while Harré carefully distinguished between formal and informal episodes, delinquency incorporates both as, in one action, the offender may be breaking state laws but following the informal rules of his friends. Thirdly, if 'rules' were to be used as a tool of analysis, greater clarity about the types of rule that young offenders follow was needed. It is helpful, at the outset of this book, to see how these problems were resolved.

Initially, it was important to establish the content and duration of the episodes under scrutiny. The nature of the delinquent's life makes this a difficult task. It might be fruitful to look at individual crimes, for example the offender's first burglary or the offence which precipitated the remand or sentence to youth custody. Particular events surrounding the offence are also of interest, such as the preparation for the crime and the reaction of the young person's family to it. The consequences of the delinquency produce a number of situations worthy of scrutiny, for instance the arrest, the court appearance and placement away from home. Focusing on one small part of the delinquent career would, however, yield limited returns. Indeed, each of the episodes just described is related to the others and, to understand the developing criminal identity, it would be more valuable to look at the combination of events experienced by offenders at different stages in their career.

In this study, therefore, an episode is defined as a variable period of time surrounding a particular phase of the delinquent career. It is well known that involvement in petty delinquency is common among young people and so this scrutiny begins later on with offenders' first participation in relatively serious crime, such as burglary and car theft. Three further episodes in the continuing career are explored. These are: being on the margins of prison when the offender is aware that further arrest or re-conviction is likely to lead to custody; the first experience of a remand or youth custody centre; and, finally, being well established in youth custody at a time when recurrent restriction of liberty is an accepted lifestyle.

Naturally, the period of time it takes to complete each episode may vary and a few young people remanded for a first offence may miss the second episode altogether. Moreover, the participants in each episode will have different criminal experiences and, indeed, one of the respondents in this research was remanded to custody for his first burglary but shared his cell with another who had twenty similar convictions but was also new to prison. The information provided by the young people will also show that the end of one episode will blend into the beginning of the next as, for instance, novices to prison rapidly become experienced in the nuances of institutional life.

Can these episodes be broken down, as Harré suggests, into those which are formal and those which are informal? Delinquency involves the contravention of some, but not all, explicit rules. The young property offenders considered in this study knowingly break certain laws and rules set down by family, teachers and, later, social workers, probation officers and magistrates. However, whether they are at liberty or in prison, the offenders' behaviour will be mostly law abiding, since it would be extremely difficult to be constantly naughty.

On the other hand, when breaking into houses, stealing cars or enduring prison life with other inmates, the young people will follow informal rules, that is those which are created and understood by those of their own age group and experience. It may be that many of these informal rules are also broken, this will be a question explored further later in this book. But it is already clear that the episodes that make up the criminal career of the forty-five young offenders under scrutiny have both formal and informal components.

Great care was taken to categorise the types of rule which young offenders are likely to follow. As has been shown, there will be formal rules guiding behaviour. The persistent delinquent is seldom a hedonist; the majority of his life at liberty will be crime free and the prison rule book will largely dictate his custodial existence. In this study, two types of formal rules are identified:

those *societal rules* which are unchanging whatever the context the young offender finds himself in and those *formal rules* which are specific to particular situations, for example court or prison.

But what kinds of informal rules will guide his existence? There will be a set of rules which guide the young person's *beliefs* about crime and prison. These rules will be in operation when he is breaking into a house, stealing a car or adapting the institutional routine to his own needs. Finally, there will be rules which guide the young offender's *interaction* with others. Not only does persistent delinquency contravene the laws of the state, it also excites disquiet amongst a number of on-lookers, many of whom will be attempting to change the young offender's lifestyle. He will need rules to guide his interaction with these people and strategies to deal with their concern for his welfare. Thus, four types of rule are identified in the following chapters; societal, formal, belief and interaction rules.

It can, therefore, be seen that some of Harré's methods can be used to understand the accounts given by the forty-five young prisoners interviewed for this study. It can be used to explore some of the concepts the young people have about themselves, particularly those concerned with their personal characteristics and social interaction. It will, in other words, help us to understand the criminal identity of these offenders. Let us explore further those aspects of the criminal identity explained using this method.

Theoretical propositions

The framework just described will reveal much about the criminal identity of young males, 15-17 years old, whose persistent delinquency has led to prison custody. Particularly important will be data which contribute to an understanding of how young people make the decisions to break into strangers' houses or to steal their cars. How do they arrive at this choice? What benefits, emotional or financial, do they perceive when they embark upon a delinquent expedition? In the early stages of the career, crime may be dismissed as adolescent experimentation, but one of the intentions of the process of capture, prosecution and conviction is to dissuade the guilty from repeating their misdemeanours. Why do these young people persist with a lifestyle the consequences of which appear to the onlooker to be uninviting and uncomfortable? These questions will be explored through episode analysis which focuses upon the rules used as a guide to criminal behaviour and provides data which break down and make clear the young offender's interpretation of events.

The role of other people in the maintenance of the criminal identity will be of interest. On the one hand there will be friends and acquaintances who participate in the criminal activity and share the criminal identity. There will be others who take an interest in the crime but who do not take part. Others, particularly members of the family, will simply be concerned that the delinquency comes to an end and/or retribution is minimal or avoided. In addition, members of the juvenile justice system, for example the police, magistrates, social workers and probation officers, will seek actively to deter the young offender from his chosen lifestyle. The criminal identity will include strategies which equip the young offender in his interaction with each of these groups and allow continuity in the chosen career. Once again, understanding the rules which guide interaction with family, friends and statutory authorities will help to fathom the different patterns of association which mark the young offender's life.

Looking at the criminal identity as a career composed of episodes and rules will also reveal inconsistencies between behaviour patterns and the way the young offender presents to the world. An external observation of a young person stealing a car, being arrested and subsequently remanded to custody in overcrowded and squalid conditions may differ markedly from the descriptions offered by one who has chosen this lifestyle and is likely to repeat the activity in the near future. Some of the rules used by the offender are likely to be contradictory at different points in the criminal career. As later chapters reveal, when the young offender first participates in relatively serious crime he shows little regard for the consequences of his actions and a gulf will be apparent between societal and belief rules. However, when he is ensconced in prison and his freedom limited, a deal of harmony becomes apparent between the rules which guide his interaction and the formal rules of the institution.

It can be seen that the method of episode analysis just described can be used to shed new light upon the criminal identity of persistent young offenders. It is useful at this point to categorise and clearly state questions about the criminal identity which can be addressed with new data from the research for this book. Working from information available from the existing criminological and social psychological literature, five theoretical propositions were developed to guide the conduct of the research. These propositions concerning choice, shared guidelines, the contribution of the juvenile justice system, the relationship of the identity to the behaviour and change in the identity over time will now be described.

To begin with, it is proposed that delinquents choose a criminal identity based upon a series of decisions which appear rational to them. This is not to say that the behaviour is rational; indeed many of the young offenders' actions will appear to lack planning and judgement and, as Rutter and Giller (1983) have noted, many delinquent acts take place in states of high emotional arousal or intoxication when rational decisions are not possible. It will, however, be possible to show that persistent delinquency makes sense to the participants. There are precedents for this proposition in studies of other deviant lifestyles, for example by Elkind (1979) and Goffman (1963). In addition to the data emerging from the episode analysis, there is evidence from other studies, such as Becker's (1963) work on jazz musicians, that individuals choose a career despite the disadvantages attendant upon the lifestyle.

Secondly, it is proposed that, in exercising his choice, the young offender uses guidelines shared with those who sympathise with his lifestyle. It may be that the first decision to steal, for example by a ten year old sneaking a chocolate bar from a supermarket, is made alone. However, during the episodes considered in this study, the delinquency is relatively serious and is likely to attract considerable hostility. The offender will need some support and guidance from others if he is to commit a burglary or car-theft. He is more likely to get involved in a criminal act if he is interacting with those who will condone his behaviour or at very least diminish the hostility of family and concerned on-lookers. Indeed, there is evidence from other studies, for example West and Farrington (eg. 1977), that a change in a delinquent's associates can lead to less involvement in crime.

The third theoretical proposition concerns the young offender's perception of the justice system and the state response to persistent delinquency. The evidence from this study will show that the justice system contributes to the young person's criminal identity. Although the justice system aims to reform criminals and deter potential delinquents, it can be counter-productive in that it brings together young people with similar criminal experiences. It will be shown that in a group of like-minded people, a young offender is able to re-interpret the experiences consequent upon particular court disposals and incorporate them into a revised identity. For example, many offenders when asked about their time in a detention centre say, 'Oh it was easy, you just do your bird and get on with it; no problem really.'

The evidence gathered on the criminal career will illustrate the impact of the juvenile justice system upon the criminal identity, which is quite distinct from criminal behaviour. The aim is not to show that care and custodial disposals engender a sense of hopelessness amongst those so sentenced, thus leading to repeated crime on release, a finding proposed by other researchers (eg. Mays 1954). Conversely, it seems that the young offender incorporates limiting life experiences as positive, necessary components of his chosen career. Again, evidence from other studies offers support for this proposition. Willis (1976), for example, describing twelve adolescent boys preparing for the dull repetition of working class life by frequent truancy, found that the school-children scorned their studious peers and made their teacher's life a misery. Even for poor performers, the education system prepares graduates for later life. The school children re-interpret their lowly position in the school and incorporate messages about lack-lustre ability into an identity which stresses machismo, strength and direction.

At the beginning of the research, it was fourthly proposed that the persistent delinquent purposively presents a criminal identity even when that identity is no longer congruent with the behaviour. For example, the young people may present to each other an image of their criminal activity as intransigent, dangerous and daring when, on closer inspection, it is revealed to be spasmodic and tame. In many cases, a delinquent gains little from his crime other than the attention it evokes among family, friends and concerned professionals. The choice of continued delinquency will have more to do with the criminal identity than any benefits, either material or emotional, to be reaped from the actual behaviour.

The divergence between behaviour and identity becomes apparent in the scrutiny of the rules used as a guide to behaviour. For example, it will be seen that once the young offender is established in a criminal career there are differences between the belief and interaction rules he uses. As he becomes more knowledgeable and skilled in his delinquency, the young offender is circumspect about how and when he will break the law. Nonetheless, he believes himself to be a delinquent and expects future arrests. As shall be seen, the frequency with which the persistent offender breaks the law decreases over time but the criminal identity becomes a constant. However, in interaction with prison and probation officers or members of his family, the young offender says he will attempt to stay within the law and 'go straight'. The belief and interaction rules convey different messages and the behaviour of the young person, which can appear conformist, becomes out of tune with the identity which remains deeply deviant.

The final theoretical proposition explored in this study is that the delinquent identity will change and develop in each of the four episodes under scrutiny. As the young offender progresses along his chosen career route, he increasingly uses rules which allow him to legitimate his delinquency in the face of condemnation from family, peers, police and courts. Despite infrequent offending, he will choose to see himself as an 'outsider' in his home community, he will feel little guilt or remorse and will begin to disengage from those whose participation in crime ends and discover a peer group who will condone and take part in his criminality. He will begin to assemble a list of rules concerned with his actual offending behaviour but struggle to put them into operation. Finally, although future years may bring a different style of life, it will be seen that, at the end of the fourth episode scrutinized for this study, the young person has fully incorporated a criminal identity.

To summarise, several proposition have been tested using the model of episode analysis previously outlined. Firstly, it is argued that the criminal identity of persistent young offenders is based upon a series of decisions which appear rational to them. Secondly, in exercising this choice, the young person uses guidelines shared with those who are sympathetic to his lifestyle. Thirdly, the juvenile justice system, despite vigorous and sometimes successful attempts to divert and deter delinquents, actually contributes to the criminal identity of the young people under scrutiny. Fourthly, the criminal identity is not always congruent with the behaviour of the young offender and, finally, the identity develops and changes with each episode in the criminal career.

Strengths and weaknesses of the study

What will this study tell us that is not already known from the literature on crime and delinquency among the young? Many themes tackled in this investigation have been pursued elsewhere. Sociologists and, less frequently, social psychologists have adopted an interactionist approach to juvenile delinquency and residential life for young people. More specifically, many studies in this mould have looked at delinquency from the perspective of the offender or at prisons from the viewpoint of the inmate. The influence of the judiciary upon delinquency has also been well charted, particularly by those who have been critical of, or have favoured, specific disposals. In addition, the influence of the wider society, its dominant values and sub-cultures upon the delinquent lifestyle, has received considerable attention and the criminal career of young offenders has been well documented. Indeed, the research team at the Cambridge Institute of Criminology traced prospectively the routes pursued by 411 schoolboys from their eighth birthday until they reached their twenty-fifth year (for example, West 1982).

This book attempts not only to pull together these approaches but also to give a new salience to the rules that influence a delinquent's behaviour and the way various key episodes assist in the development of the criminal identity. In so doing, it will address aspects of the delinquent career which can seem contradictory, for example carrying on with crime despite the absence of material rewards and the pains of imprisonment. Furthermore, these theoretical observations will be illustrated by existential descriptions of various aspects of the criminal career not explored by other writers, for example the excitement of crime and the fright of the first few days in prison. Themes from a variety of studies have been brought together using methods novel to the subject area and which can be used systematically to interpret empirically observed aspects of the young offender's lifestyle. Thus, whilst the individual components of the study have been well tried, they have not previously been brought together in a single theoretical model.

However, it must also be emphasised that the interactionist approach and method applied in this study is only one of many ways of understanding crime and delinquency. Moreover, adopting an interactionist stance does not result in a causal explanation of delinquency. Nonetheless, the research findings contribute towards the several causal chains and processes which Rutter and Giller (1983) identify as contributing towards juvenile delinquency. Furthermore, the information collected from young people helps to explain why individuals who do not display any unique psychological traits continue with deviant behaviour which is apparently unrewarding.

2. Understanding young people's interpretations

In this chapter, the theoretical perspective and method for explaining social behaviour in this study are described. The principal component of this approach is 'rules' which guide social action. Other writers who have used this tool of analysis are discussed. A scheme developed by Harré and Secord is examined and clarified in the light of a critique of their work by Argyle. Further criticisms offered by other social theorists are put forward. Finally, the general and specific principles of a framework for understanding young people's interpretations of their situation are outlined.

It is intended to explore the young offender's interpretation of his situation at different stages in the criminal career. There are many sociological methods available for this purpose. Some, for example participant observation, would be extremely difficult to organise in a prison. Others, such as non-participant observation and interviews are less problematic. However, in studies which rely upon individuals' accounts, there is a danger of amassing a series of interview transcripts which overwhelm the investigation. This chapter describes a way of structuring qualitative material collected in the remand and youth custody centre participating in this study.

The chosen perspective builds upon the work of Rom Harré and other psychologists who have followed the principles of investigation laid down in the study *The Explanation of Social Behaviour.* Harré's approach is fully explained together with a more detailed look at ways in which 'rules' of behaviour have been used to understand social life. There have been several criticisms of Harré's work and these have been most helpful in arriving at a method applicable to the study in hand, particularly those suggested by Michael Argyle. Let us begin with a description of Harré's approach to the explanation of social behaviour.

Harré's approach to the understanding of social behaviour

In a series of books and articles Rom Harré has espoused a theoretical perspective and method which challenge traditional social psychological approaches to social behaviour (eg. Harré and Secord 1972, Harré 1978, Harré 1979, Harré, Clarke and De Carlo 1985). Harré and Secord (1972) begin their work with a series of criticisms of commonly employed research methods used by social psychologists on the grounds that they force the subjects under investigation into a passive role and reduce complex liaisons to simple equations, thus losing the quality of the interaction. Mechanistic models of social behaviour which emphasise causal explanations are rejected in favour of techniques which seek deeper understanding of human action and which have been compared by other psychologists with literature, biography and journalism.

The approach preferred by Harré and Secord (1972) is referred to as an anthropomorphic model of man in which people are treated for scientific purposes 'as if they were human beings'. Those championing the interpretive methods used by sociologists, principally ethnomethodology and hermeneutics, find many features in common with Harré's work (see Shutz 1970, Winch 1958, Garfinkel 1967, Silverman 1970). The new approach stresses the importance of language, both verbal and non-verbal, between individuals. It puts emphasis upon the way individuals perceive, interpret and create situations. The focus is upon the meaning in actors' actions, that is the purpose of their behaviour, and the intentions of actors, that is to say the goals they seek to achieve.

Harré and Secord (1972) further espouse the benefits of an approach to understanding social behaviour which represents a co-operative venture between psychologists, philosophers and sociologists. As the authors note, each discipline is ill-equipped to tackle the subject area alone.

> Psychologists have often been concerned with too narrow a conception of social action and have been severely handicapped by conceptual naivete. Philosophers have not lacked in conceptual sophistication but have too often been ignorant of social and psychological facts, while sociologists, despite great breadth of conception, have been unable to develop adequate theories of individual social action and have suffered, with psychologists, from conceptual naivete.

It is proposed by Harré, and others using similar methods, that in analysing social behaviour it is fruitful to look at particular events or episodes and to scrutinize the rules guiding people's actions in these episodes. As has been seen, rules are defined by Harré as propositions which guide social action through participants being aware of the rules and their prescriptions. However, rules have been used as a conceptual device for exploring social behaviour by a variety of writers from a range of disciplines. Let us look more closely at the use of 'rules' by the social sciences.

Rules of behaviour

The use of rules as a tool to understand social behaviour is common to anthropology, linguistics, philosophy, psychology and sociology. Many well known academics have been concerned to fashion concepts of rules, including Malinowski, Chomsky, Wittgenstein, Piaget and Winch. There is, however, confusion over the use of the concept. Often it is thought of as a norm of behaviour which is conspicuous by its regularity or because it has been legitimated by the local culture (Parsons, Bales and Shils, 1951). Alternatively, it is taken to mean the role expected of an individual in a particular setting (Mead 1934).

Sociologists have preferred the concept of 'norm' to 'rule'. Human behaviour is subject to regular patterns which can be viewed as the logical outcome of individuals following norms or common expectations. Lambert, Millham and Bullock (1970) have defined a norm as 'a common standard which guides and defines the limits of members' responses in an established group'. The term usually refers to social expectations about correct behaviour in specified social situations and, as such, implies the presence of legitimacy, consent and prescription. Deviations from normative patterns are usually punished by sanctions.

Philosophers and psychologists have been more concerned with rules of behaviour. Generally, a rule is a conceptual device for understanding what human beings mean when they communicate with each other. Rules guide behaviour and can be important in determining expectations of future behaviour but their authority is doubtful and there are seldom sanctions to chastise those who do not concur. This flexible use of the rules of behaviour militates against their value for aetiological explanations of human behaviour.

Some who have studied rules of behaviour distinguish between various levels at which rules affect our lives. Kant made the distinction between 'regulative' rules, those which regulate or guide behaviour, and 'constitutive' rules, which define or constitute human action (Quinne 1972). Rules underpin and guide social behaviour, but it would be wrong to assume that they are static or unchanging. Indeed, de Saussure (1974) found a significant difference between the rules of social practices and institutions as they exist at any one time, and the rules of social practice and institutions which are subject to change.

In philosophy, an important distinction has been drawn between the differing nature of rules, for example do they govern social action or are they loose guides which can be ignored? (eg. Black 1972, Gumb 1972, Marsh, Rosser and Harré 1978) Empirical researchers tend to emphasise the guiding influence of rules, if only because data do not easily lend themselves to causal explanations. It is possible to observe regularities in social episodes but their form and outcome are very difficult to predict. These empiricists are given support by Wittgenstein (1958) who stated that 'rules leave room for doubt'.

> We can easily imagine people amusing themselves in a field by playing with a ball so as to start various existing games, but playing without finishing them and in between throwing the ball aimlessly in the air, chasing one another with the ball and bombarding one another for a joke and so on. And now someone says: The whole time they are playing a game and following very definite rules at every throw

The context of such doubt is complicated as rules are not only optional to individuals in particular episodes but they may also change over time, instance de Saussure's (1974) finding that the component rules of social practices differ from one moment to another. In addition, rules may be used in different ways by different cultures. Anthropologists have found that rules underpinning tribal negotiations operate differently from one society to another.

Consequently, it is unlikely that the discovery of rules will help to predict delinquency, neither will it reveal the causes of young people's continuing criminal life-style. Indeed, once the rules have been identified it will be difficult to assess the extent to which they are followed or the exact moments when they will apply. However, as the anthropologist Malinowski (1963) has shown, the extent and mechanisms of deviations from stated rules are the most important part of the researcher's task. Just because a rule is broken or does not apply to a particular situation does not discount its value to the investigator.

As in a child's game, in life people sometimes make up the rules as they go along or alter them to suit their immediate needs. But this perspective fits well with the general mess of young offenders' lives. Adolescents appear to set few limits to each others' behaviour and sometimes act in relatively strange ways, but this does not mean that they act wantonly. Persistent delinquents break laws and, possibly, social expectations of family and friends, but this does not mean that there is no structure to their behaviour. Close scrutiny reveals underlying regularities and the rules of criminal and delinquent behaviour help us to understand the developing criminal identity of young people.

In summary, rules are generally understood to provide a framework for social behaviour, they have an undoubted influence upon the final form of individual conduct, but are continuously adapted and changed by the participants during each social episode.

Criticisms of Harré's methods

Having described Harré's approach to the study of social behaviour and given more detailed information about the use of rules as a tool of analysis for social scientists, it is valuable to consider the criticisms of Harré's work, a task aided by Michael Argyle's (1978) appraisal of the stance. Argyle finds four strengths and weaknesses in Harré's position.

Firstly, Argyle agrees with Harré that traditional research methods used by psychologists have been too artificial and are subject to errors in the collection of data. Thus, any approach which will supplement existing tools of analysis are to be welcomed. Secondly, the emphasis upon the cognitions of the individual has led to an improved understanding of actors' behaviour and new methods of cognitive testing. Thirdly, Harré's approach has stimulated research new to psychology, for example Marsh's (1978) work on the rules which manage apparent disorder on football terraces and Rosser's finding that school children have rules to which they expect teachers to keep (Marsh, Rosser and Harré 1978). Fourthly, Argyle welcomes the new approach in that a model of social life is put forward which has more in common with everyday experience.

On the other hand, Argyle finds several weaknesses in Harré's theoretical perspective and method. To begin with, although it is presented almost as a new paradigm, in that it rejects previous methods as inappropriate to social science, it does not 'explain' these traditional ideas. Argyle questions the value of abandoning this body of material and, in his second criticism of Harré's work, claims that cross-fertilisation between the old and the new would bear more fruit. The present position wherein traditional methodologists reject participant observation and interviewing whilst the new theorists adopt these methods but reject all else is unsatisfactory. Argyle calls for a combination of existing causal designs with the new cognitive methods and, as an example, puts forward his own preferred approach. Let us briefly consider Argyle's position.

Traditionally, psychology, like sociology, has adopted logical positivism as the philosophical basis of investigation; social beings are treated as natural phenomena and scrutiny focuses upon the relationship between living 'organisms'. Argyle has been more flexible in that he recognizes the importance of cultural factors in social behaviour including individuals' definitions of social acts and rules. He also realises the importance of the historical development of these definitions and rules. However, some aspects of social behaviour can be explained as biological processes and it is important to map out all of the main variables which may explain different types of social behaviour. Thus, for Argyle, Harré's emphasis upon cognitive processes has only part of the answer to the problems of investigation in the social sciences.

The third criticism of Harré's method concerns its exclusive emphasis on individuals' accounts. There are, says Argyle, important limits to our knowledge of people's meanings and perceptions. For example, although Harré assumes that individuals act intentionally, people are often surprised when they watch a videotape of themselves in action. Furthermore, although people may act with the intention of fulfilling particular goals, they can often engender from others exactly the opposite of their desired response. For a number of reasons, accounts can be viewed as unreliable and should be treated with caution when they are the principal source of information for researchers.

Finally, Argyle attacks the complexity of the philosophical debate forwarded by Harré, noting that many of the arguments are insoluble. He argues that traditional psychological research, with its emphasis upon empirical data, is, in many cases, far more beneficial than novel philosophical musing. Rules, notes Argyle, are useful tools with which to interpret participants' explanations of the behaviour under study, but they do not provide comprehensive knowledge and relentless pursuit of their nature can lead to needless complication. This caveat is most useful for, if the inmates' perspective is to be emphasised, it will be important not to obscure their intentions by the chosen method of analysis.

Generally, Argyle welcomes the new ideas piloted and tested by Harré. The critique is best summed up in the following quotation in which Argyle claims that Harré and his disciples have

> gone too far in the abandonment of procedures and verification, in giving up hope of discovering useful generalisations, and in rejecting nearly everything that has gone before. I believe that their main doctrines can be incorporated in a broadened but still rigorous kind of social science.

A sociological critique

What other weaknesses can be found in the approach of Rom Harré? For the sociologist, there is a need to relate details about an individual's social life to more structural social processes. Sociologists have conducted a great deal of research into institutional life which has attempted to associate formal and informal social systems. Does the use of rules by sociologists help with an understanding of the relationship between individual social action and the wider society?

The deepest scrutiny of the link between culture and the social structure is still that of Merton (1938, 1957) who found that individuals internalise goals during their cognitive development. These goals are set against socially constructed rules which guide and limit behaviour. In Merton's model, rules are both normative and regulative in nature. For many people, particularly those who have few life chances, there is a 'strain' between internalised goals and the social rules of behaviour. The majority, in Merton's view, conform to internalised goals but a minority select a variety of deviant adaptations including 'innovation', the illegitimate attainment of cultural goals, and 'rebellion', in which the offender rejects the status quo and replaces it with an alternative set of goals. Thus, Merton provides one useful model which attempts to relate rules of behaviour to the wider social system.

In a series of books and articles, successive members of the team at the Dartington Social Research Unit have sought to understand and relate the informal and formal social systems in residential communities. Their work has considerable relevance to those who seek to identify informal and formal rules of behaviour. Lambert, Millham and Bullock (1973) showed that there are many types of relationship between the informal and formal social system; inmates can be supportive, manipulative, passive and rejecting of the formal goals of the institution. Similarly, whilst the informal system can help to ease the pains of imprisonment, Millham, Bullock and Cherrett (1972) found that it can also be brutal and, for the sake of maintaining an informal hierarchy, foster violence. It should not be assumed in the coming pages that this informal system is cosy and warm.

Indeed, the complex relationship between the informal and formal social world of a residential institution is found to be reflected in institutional goals. If the norms of the informal system reflect formal goals then other similarities, for example in control, between the two systems will follow. Thus, a change in the methods of formal control can often change methods of coercion in the informal system and it is possible to decrease the violence amongst inmates by reducing injuries inflicted by the institution upon its members. However, if the goals of the informal system reject the goals of the formal system, then it follows that the residential centre's ability to influence the inmates will be less straightforward.

The relationship between formal and informal goals is clearest in Dartington's study of boarding schools. The public school experience is part of a clear career structure which will propel graduates into University, the City, public service and other worthy positions within society. As such, deviance, sexual or criminal, is tolerated as it is functional to the institution. The deviance contributes to the smooth running of the public school for it channels loyalties, lusts and an enormous amount of effort into activities which do not challenge the formal system of the institution; indeed, it can be viewed as highly committed behaviour. Moreover, Lambert, Bullock and Millham (1975) have found that the informal world of the public school and the way senior boys have continuously to exert control by balancing the needs of the formal and informal system provides crucial training for an administrator required to reconcile public and private divisions. It is possible to see how continuities in social careers are possible, a theme explored in some depth in the coming pages.

A clear finding to emerge from this study is the way in which young prisoners negotiate society's response to their delinquency. As shall be seen, certain avenues of the criminal career are provided by the state. The rules which allow a young prisoner to adapt, to create an acceptable lifestyle and formulate new goals will clearly reflect the wider social structure. Other models relating informal and formal social systems which expand the perspectives of Merton and the Dartington team will be explored as the study progresses. These will supplement the method for understanding young people's interpretations which will now be outlined.

A framework for understanding young people's interpretations

The theoretical perspective and method of understanding the accounts given by the subjects of social research put forward by Harré and Secord (1972), the discussion on the use of rules as a conceptual tool for the social sciences and the critique of Harré's work by Michael Argyle (1978) have been used to develop a framework for understanding young people's interpretations of their situation. This framework is best outlined in two parts, firstly the general principles of investigation and, secondly, the specific way in which the method is applied to understanding interviews with young people in the remand and youth custody centre participating in this study.

1) General principles

As was described in the opening chapter this study focuses upon four episodes in the delinquent career; the first participation in relatively serious crime such as burglary; life on the margins of prison when further arrest or re-conviction is likely to lead to custody; the first experience of prison; and, the episode during which continued restriction of liberty is an accepted part of the young offender's lifestyle.

These episodes have no distinct beginning and end. They represent variable but usually broad periods of time surrounding a particular phase in the delinquent career. The episodes scrutinized in this study have both formal and informal rules as the delinquent breaks some, but not all, of the state laws and adheres to rules which guide the more equivocal aspects of his behaviour. From prisoners' accounts of their behaviour in each episode, four types of rule are identified.

Initially, any analysis must take into account societal rules which change little over time and are as true in prison as they are outside in the community. For instance, the rule which states that it is wrong to steal applies throughout the criminal career. However, many of the societal rules will be adapted to the particular context the offender finds himself in and it will be possible to identify a second set of formal rules which are specific to, for example, the police station and the prison. Thirdly, there will be belief rules which will guide the offender's view of his predicament at various points in time. Finally, there is another group of interaction rules which will guide the offender in his liaisons throughout the criminal career. The societal rules will remain constant throughout the career, but the others will change.

The discussion of rules in this chapter has led to a clear definition of the concept as it will be used in this study. Rules provide a framework for social behaviour, they have an undoubted influence upon the final form of individual conduct but they are continuously adapted and changed during each social episode. Each of the societal, formal, belief and interaction rules identified in this study will adhere to this definition.

Argyle has noted that there is a question-mark over research which relies solely upon participants' statements so, where possible, other checks and balances have been built into this research design. For example, it is possible to observe some of the social episodes that contribute to the criminal career, such as time spent in prison. Furthermore, more precise methods have been used to create a better understanding of patterns of interaction. These will augment and act as a check against the prisoners' perspective.

Using the method of splitting the criminal career into its component episodes and rules has made it possible in this study to relate formal and informal social systems in a novel way. Over time, the congruity between societal, formal, belief and interaction rules available to the young people under scrutiny is likely to change. For example, during the early episodes when crime can be viewed as adolescent experimentation, the belief rules are likely to be congruous with interaction rules as the delinquent freely describes the event to his peers and plays down its importance. During the first days in prison, however, interaction rules will be most congruous with the formal rules of the prison as the inmate draws comfort from the institutional routine. Other parallels and discontinuities between informal and formal social systems will become apparent using the methods outlined in this chapter.

2) Specific application of the method

It is now possible briefly to outline the specific method adopted in this study for understanding young offenders' interpretation of their situation at various points in the criminal career. More detailed information about the research design, for example interviewing techniques and numbers participating in the study are offered in the following chapter. Here the concern is simply to describe how rules of behaviour are identified from young offenders' descriptions of their criminal career.

Initially, young property offenders resident in the remand centre and youth custody centre were interviewed, using an open-ended instrument, about a variety of aspects of their criminal career. The interview schedule was designed in the light of other research findings about juvenile delinquency and prison life. The information collected from the young people was retrospective, relying upon prisoners looking back one to three years over their life as persistent property offenders. In order to gauge the accuracy of the data, inmates were first interviewed individually and then in groups of five. Furthermore, other techniques such as analysis of group dynamics and non-participant observation allowed for more checks upon the validity of the information collected.

The data were then transcribed and categorized into the four episodes of the criminal career looked at in this study; the first participation in relatively serious crime; life on the margins of prison; the first experience of prison; and, finally, continued restriction of liberty. The principal components of each episode were then identified and form the basis of this book.

In cases where there was some doubt over the principal components of episodes, for example where interviews produced very varied material or where information was insufficiently comprehensive, further interviews were conducted. From all of this information the societal, formal, belief and interaction rules operating in each of the four episodes under scrutiny were identified using a procedure described in the next chapter. These rules were then listed and are given in the chapters describing the findings of the research.

Ideally, it should be possible to test further whether these rules operate in the early criminal career of property offenders. This would involve a prospective scrutiny of a large study cohort who would be asked to identify from a full list of rules those which may operate at various points in the criminal career. However, the resources were not available for a study of this size and type. Moreover, statistical validation would be further hampered by the definition of rules outlined above; if a majority of the sample did not identify a rule as operating at a particular point in time, this would not deny the value of the rule as a guide to behaviour. In any case, this study does not claim to offer a causal explanation with sophisticated statistical procedures. The framework for understanding young people's interpretations just described is a conceptual device for a more systematic analysis of what people mean and intend when they describe their actions.

Summary Points

1. A novel way of understanding young people's interpretations has been outlined. This method builds upon a perspective developed by Rom Harré.
2. Harré has put forward an interpretive approach which focuses upon the meaning in participants' actions, that is the purpose of their behaviour, the intentions of actors and the goals they seek to achieve. Harré's method separates social action into episodes and focuses upon the rules operating in that episode.
3. Various disciplines have used the concept of 'rules' to explain social action. The term is an attractive tool of analysis in that it accounts for the unpredictability in human behaviour. However, this flexibility militates against the use of rules in aetiological explanations.
4. Rules are defined as providing a framework for social behaviour which have an undoubted influence upon the final form of individual conduct but which are continuously adapted and clarified during each social episode.
5. Argyle puts forward four strengths and four weaknesses of Harré's approach. Generally, the view is proposed that the new perspective goes too far in abandoning existing procedures. Argyle views Harré's approach as most valuable when used in combination with established causal methods.
6. For the sociologist, the method is welcomed as an additional way of linking informal and formal social systems. Research has linked the formal and informal social systems of residential institutions. This relationship is complex; it depends upon the degree of consensus amongst the informal group, the strength of its informal control and its pervasiveness.
7. The method used in this study for understanding young people's interpretations has been outlined. The criminal career is separated into four episodes. Four types of rule operating in each episode are identified from interviews with young people resident in a remand and youth custody centre.

3. Research design

In this chapter a research design is described. Four strategies and their inherent problems are discussed; file analysis; interviews with young prisoners; non-participant observation; and analysis of group dynamics. The various contributions to the project of remand and youth custody centre boys are outlined.

Having dealt with the general methodological approach used in this book, it is possible to describe the research design for collecting information from the remand and youth custody centre participating in this study. At the outset of the research, it was decided to collect new data from residents at a remand and youth custody centre, two institutions central to the criminal career of the young people under scrutiny. Although a majority of those interviewed had previously been to detention centres, a remand to custody represents an important step in the young offender's experience of prison department custody. The research is primarily concerned with the less experienced property offender who finds his way to prison custody, enabling the fieldwork in the remand centre to focus upon accommodation sheltering those aged less than 18 years. Placement in a youth custody centre is the principal form of detention for young offenders, so this type of institution was also seen as an important source of information.

Prison research of any kind is fraught with difficulties, but the nature of this study incurs additional methodological problems. The prison is the common denominator for the young people under scrutiny, yet prisoners are transitory, oscillating between institutions and their home or community relatively quickly. The research, therefore, seeks information from inmates about a range of situations, not just the prison.

In this chapter, an outline is given of a variety of methods, including analysis of data stored in prison records, interviews with inmates, non-participant observation and study of group dynamics. Moreover, the number of prisoners participating in the various components of the design is charted. Let us begin, however, with a review of the difficulties encountered by researchers' studies in prisons.

Difficulties in prison research

The difficulties of conducting social research in public organisations have been poorly considered. Martin Bulmer (1982) focused on the conflict between organisational needs and academic interests, difficulties which are particularly pressing in prison and exacerbated by additional problems of ethics and confidentiality. For example, Clarke and Cornish (1975) discovered several conflicts of interest faced by researchers working for the Home Office. Cohen and Taylor (1972) conducted an independent study in the maximum security wing of Durham prison and are particularly critical of the constraints placed on them by the Home Office (Cohen and Taylor 1975 and 1977). The Durham research exposes the problems created by an approach which shows empathy for the prisoners rather than for the feelings of prison officers, governors and government departments.

King and Elliott (1977) have suggested a range of roles previously adopted by prison researchers, each incurring particular difficulties. There are those who enter the institution independent of government funding or influence on research findings, such as the study of Pentonville by Pauline and Terence Morris (1963). Other work, for example Emery (1970), is directly sponsored by the Home Office. Cohen and Taylor's (1972) scrutiny of Durham prison displayed a mutual prisoner and research interest, but in Bottoms and McClintock's (1973) report on Dover borstal the emphasis was shared between research and prison staff.

In practice, the researcher often adopts a variety of roles. This book is based on independent research; it was not officially sponsored but it was vetted by the Home Office and is intended to be of benefit to research, prisoners and prison staff alike. Indeed, in developing research methods for this study, great care was taken to avoid organisational and political problems. The process of gaining access to many residential centres, particularly prisons is, as one would expect, delicate. Decisions to allow entry and scrutiny of daily practice are not taken lightly and careful negotiation took place at every level. The Home Office, the governors, the Prison Officers' Association, the chief and principal officers, the prisoners and their parents were all consulted in connection with this study and, without exception, they were all extremely co-operative and helpful.

Nonetheless, in a prison there are many practical constraints on research design. Unless one commits an offence it is not possible to become a participant observer, interviews and questionnaires have to be arranged and constructed with great care and the information they produce is subject to strict ethical controls. Furthermore, each individual visit to the prison has to be carefully arranged and timed. It is not possible to stroll around closed institutions at one's leisure.

Where prison is the focus of investigation, it is best to treat the institution as a small community in which members have different and competing interests. Over-association with particular individuals, for example the governor or the chief officer, could prejudice the participation of the inmates or even that of other officers. There is also a danger of being taken over by the institution. For example, people who have worked long in a particular setting often have well-considered and interesting research perspectives which can easily side-track the investigator.

The research took into account the dangers of a Hawthorne effect, that the investigation may change the regime under study, although the possibility of such an occurrence in a prison is minimal. More importantly, great efforts were made to make clear to participants the confidentiality of information offered to the researcher. Prisoners and prison officers alike were told that interview material would not be made available to anybody else in the institution nor to the prison department.

Just as great care has to be taken in establishing an independent research role, consideration is needed when disengaging from the institution. Particularly important is to avoid building up people's expectations about the research and to make clear to participants the time it will take to analyse the data and prepare a report.

It can be seen that conducting research within prisons is not without its difficulties. However, given the importance of the institution to the careers of persistent property offenders, it was the best place to collect information. Nonetheless, in arriving at an appropriate research design, care was taken to focus upon the entire criminal career and not just the time spent in custody.

Working from the principles of episode analysis described in the previous chapter and taking into account the constraints of prison research just described, four strands of investigation were considered necessary in the search for information about the criminal identity of young offenders remanded or sentenced to custody. Initially, evidence was gathered on prisoners' backgrounds and criminal careers from the records kept in the institution. However, the principal source of information was a series of interviews with inmates, individually and in groups of five. Time spent in the remand and the youth custody centre was also used as an opportunity to observe the prisoner interaction and the day-to-day working of the institution. Finally, in order to gather more concrete evidence on patterns of interaction and hierarchy, a sub-study analysing the dynamics of groups of prisoners was mounted.

Let us look further at the components of this design and iron out any difficulties that arise.

File analysis

There are theoretical strengths and weaknesses in the use of official statistics (Belson and Hood 1967). However, most institutions assemble a range of files and records on residents and, in prisons in England and Wales, almost every detail of a prisoner's daily routine comes under scrutiny at one time or another. Moreover, many of the young people in this study will have passed through a number of institutions and, as a result, there is a plethora of biographical data, much of which is relevant to the study in hand.

Official records are not, however, the most reliable sources from which to draw information (Hindess 1973). Firstly, they are usually based upon interviews involving people whose interests do not co-incide. Secondly, they are collected by numerous agencies, for example the police and the courts, each of which has particular aims, objectives and idiosyncrasies. Thirdly, the method of data collection may differ from area to area. For example, the court records of a young person who has served a detention centre order in Gloucestershire may differ from another imprisoned in Leicestershire, although they share a remand cell in the West Midlands.

Not only are prison records unreliable, they also lack insight. Whatever the subject matter, be it daily routine, a breach of prison discipline or a list of previous offences, the bare minimum of information is collected. It is against this background that the validity of such information should be judged.

Nonetheless, files cataloguing movement both within and between institutions are particularly useful for this study. The record of previous convictions lists the date(s), offence(s) and court appearance(s) for each successful prosecution against the young person. By recording this information for all young people resident in the youth custody centre or wing of the remand centre at the time of scrutiny and placing it upon a graph to map the year of offence and time spent in an institution, it is possible retrospectively to trace the prison and court careers of the inmates.

Movement also occurs within institutions. Prisoners on remand are often transferred daily from one cell to another. Their exact location at any one time is recorded by prison officers and forms a useful source of data for the analysis of group dynamics and hierarchies. In youth custody, detainees share dormitories rather than cells and enjoy relative liberty, making movement more difficult to detect. Nonetheless, it will be interesting to see whether prisoners who share age, offence histories or geographical background gravitate towards one another.

In addition to providing valuable information on the characteristics and geographical background of inmates, the prison files have helped further in the charting of criminal careers and patterns of interaction among persistent property offenders held in youth custody. Let us now turn to the principal component of the research design, interviews with the inmates.

Interviews

In order to know how young prisoners interpret their situation at various points in the criminal career, it is necessary to interview them. Ideally, the interviews should be conducted as the career develops, but the available resources and problems of building up a cohort dictate that the information presented here will be retrospective. What are the difficulties and problems interviews are likely to throw up and how can these be overcome?

Discussions on the merits of interviewing focus both on the conduct of the interview and the validity of the information revealed. For example, Woods (1986) notes that interviews ought to be 'democratic, two-way, informal, free-flowing processes' and Glaser and Strauss (1967) note that key respondents, individuals who capture a disproportionate amount of the researchers' interest, can badly distort the picture portrayed by a chosen sample of respondents.

In conducting interviews it is important for the interviewer to appear independent (Measor 1985). As discussed earlier, Cohen and Taylor chose to side with the inmates in the conduct of their study, a strategy which can antagonise prison staff. For the younger inmate, the prison officer is likely to be an integral part of his life and there is nothing to be gained by siding with one group or another. Clearly, the quality of information will suffer if the inmates view the researcher as a part of the prison organisation, so great care is required to establish an independent role in which the prisoner can have confidence.

Ball (1983), finds that it is often easier for the interviewer than the interviewee to engage in an open discussion and, as Stenhouse (1984) notes, conditions have to be carefully created to give the interviewee an opportunity to tell the world his or her particular view on life. Hammersley and Atkinson (1983) have shown that research interviews are similar, in many ways, to other forms of social interaction and that both researcher and respondent play a part in structuring the dialogue.

In interviewing inmates at the remand and the youth custody centre, great care was taken to avoid key respondents who might distort overall findings and, in total, 45 inmates were questioned at length. A long time was spent in each institution establishing an independent role and encouraging inmates to feel confident enough to participate in the study. Conditions for interviewing in prison, an unused cell or room, are not ideal and are difficult to negotiate, but by conducting the discussion over a period of days and inviting groups of inmates to be re-interviewed, a fairly relaxed atmosphere was achieved.

In day to day interaction with each other we move swiftly and easily from one subject to another. However, there are difficulties for the researcher who must encourage the free-flow of speech, yet keep hold of any questions that arise. For example, the following extract about a youngster's first burglary throws up a number of questions which might fruitfully be pursued.

'I was wagging school, and we had about 15p. And we wanted these pies from the bakery, they was about 40p and 50p. So we didn't know what to do to get them or anything, but we saw a house and I said, "Shall we have a go?" and he says, "Yeh". So I says, "Go and knock at the door and see if anybody's in". So he went to the door and nobody was in. So these three kids went round the back and I was keeping watch. And they smashed a window, I heard this window smash, and I was waiting about five minutes, but it seemed like an hour. So I went round and got into the house and started searching after that. Robbed £90 out of a glass. And I just started doing more after that.'

During the interview the researcher must reflect upon and pursue at least another nine and possibly many more items, all of which are worthy of further discussion. These are; wagging school; the importance of the discrepancy between the cost of pies and the money the boys had; why it was that particular house they 'saw'; the inconsistency of the numbers involved; the apparent passivity of his contribution; the time dimension (it seemed like an hour); what were they searching for; the distribution and use of the £90 and the subsequent burglaries.

The question of validity is more thorny. How can the researcher be sure that respondents are not distorting the truth, telling out-right lies or exaggerating a point? This problem is accentuated when there is a limited amount of time allocated to fieldwork and the number of interviews is restricted. Moreover, distortions in participants' accounts have been a particular problem for this study as the young prisoners' ability to distort the truth is one of the central theoretical propositions being explored. If it is accepted that young prisoners actively deceive, is it possible to rely upon the evidence generated by interviews?

To begin with, the use of a research technique which gives the respondent room to fabricate a truth may tell the investigator more about the interviewee's culture than more structured techniques. As Hammersley and Atkinson (1983) have found, what qualitative interviews lose in terms of accuracy of data is usually balanced by the insights gained into the lifestyle of the person being interviewed.

Secondly, it should not be assumed that distortion will easily deceive the interviewer, particularly if he or she is well-versed in the subject matter. As Whyte (1982) found, the plausibility of accounts can be checked during the interview, old ground can be re-turned, information constantly checked. If there remain problems, the interviewer can arrange further meetings with the respondent at a later date. Indeed, by adopting the Glaser and Strauss (1967) proposal that interviewees should be chosen on the basis of theoretical sampling, it is possible further to alleviate difficulties. Theoretical sampling involves changing the questions and respondents according to the current state of knowledge within the research project. This method avoids individuals' providing the definitive answer to a particular question.

These strategies are quite sufficient for checking the validity of accounts, particularly when 45 prisoners are interviewed. In addition, and in order to expose distortion, a further sub-sample of inmates was re-interviewed in groups of five. The relationship between information released in group and individual interviews is most important. The groups act as a check upon the information volunteered by individuals and questions to a prisoner repeated in the presence of a group of inmates can reveal inconsistency. Gold (1966) used a similar technique when he checked the validity of subjects' accounts with their friends. The nature and quality of the contradictions are the key to this study as they tell us which aspects of behaviour can be exaggerated or lied about and the ability of inmates to relay confusing messages about their behaviour.

The majority of interviews with inmates were tape-recorded. In cases where inmates objected or where the conditions were not right for tape-recording, notes were taken. The data collected were transcribed and categorized into each of the four episodes as described in the preceding chapter. This further helped to overcome the problem of key respondents dominating qualitative research reports. None of the transcripts remained in one part, they were each cut and pasted into the relevant study categories.

In the following chapters, examples of the rules of behaviour operating in each of the episodes are listed. How were these lists of rules arrived at? Once the interviews were categorized into the various episodes and the principal components of these episodes were established, the information was again surveyed and the societal, formal, belief and interaction rules of behaviour were identified. Initially, any rule which appeared to be operating in a particular episode was listed even if the data supporting its presence were scanty. Further interviews clarified points of ambiguity. The interview material was searched again and rules eliminated if doubts over their existence persisted. In cases where many rules in a particular category were apparent, the list was ended at the point where additional information added little to the research findings. As the preceding chapter illustrated, it was not possible to apply further statistical analysis as another check of validity.

The categorized interview material and the lists of rules of behaviour acted as the basis for the following chapters outlining the findings from the young people resident in the remand and the youth custody centre. Once the chapters were written, quotations from interviews were chosen which best illustrated the points in the discussion and ten rules from each category are given as examples of the overall findings.

To summarise, from a series of interviews with inmates, retrospective information on their criminal careers was gathered. In order to encourage confidence and open discussion a considerable time was taken to establish with prisoners and prison officers an independent role. Finally, care was taken to monitor but not discourage distortion in participants' accounts. Inconsistencies were revealed by re-interviewing individuals in groups of five, by careful analysis of the interview material and, where necessary, conducting further interviews with prisoners and prison officers.

Let us now turn to another complementary approach to gathering fresh data, non-participant observation.

Non-participant observation

An ideal way to collect information about interaction in prison would be to live in the institutions and follow prisoners on release. The benefits of this approach can be judged by the insights provided by prison graduates such as Brendan Behan (1958) on borstals, John McVicar (1979) on long term imprisonment, Bruno Bettelheim (1960) on the ravages of a Nazi concentration camp, Alexander Solzhenitsyn (1968) on the extremes of Siberian labour camps or Jimmy Boyle (1977) on a therapeutic community within a maximum security jail. All lived within the environment they describe and their writings have a quality quite unlike mainstream research.

Not surprisingly, a large chunk of writing about research methods has concentrated on the ways in which researchers can obtain data of this quality (Giddens 1976, Denzin 1970, Filstead 1970, Hammersley and Atkinson 1983). Most are at pains to show that the researcher can become a member of the group under observation without affecting its structure, an approach known as participant observation (Becker 1958, Becker and Geer 1960). In prison, it would be extremely difficult, if not impossible, to be a participant observer and slip unobtrusively into the inmate group. Nevertheless, the principles and aims of the method have obvious attractions and there is a viable alternative in non-participant observation (Woods 1986).

Non-participant observation can be defined as 'participant observation where the group under scrutiny is aware of the researcher's role'. The researcher may change the dynamics of the group but the effect can be minimized as participants become acquainted with and feel at ease with the stranger.

During research for this book, considerable time was spent in prison with prisoners, especially during the preparation and conduct of interviews with 45 young people. Notes made on inmates' daily interaction and the experience of being in the institution proved to be invaluable informants as well as becoming a further check upon interview material. Indeed, early on in the study, non-participation observation suggested that inmates were organised in a hierarchical fashion, but that participants assumed different roles in the structure according to the particular focus of the group. In order to test this possibility, a further sub-study was mounted using established techniques to measure group dynamics.

Group dynamics

There have been various schools of sociology and psychology which have been concerned with measuring interaction. In sociology the main proponents have been the ethnomethodologists whilst psychology has been more successful in developing specific measures of the dynamics of group interaction.

Fundamentally, group dynamics analysis concentrates on interpretation and subsequent categorisation of individual utterances made by participants. Bales (1950), for example, categorizes the contribution made by group members into four 'task areas': positive reactions, attempted answers, questions and negative reactions. By coding utterances into this scheme,

Bales attempted to reveal the dynamics of the group under scrutiny including its leaders and followers.

Building upon this base, Carter (1954) and Bales (1958) identified three principal differences between members of a group. These are; activity, the frequency of contributions to the conversation; task ability, their skill in responding to questions posed by other members; and likeability, whether the individual presents well to other participants. Activity is measured by the frequency of an individual's contribution to the group, including non-verbal communication. Task ability is measured by members rating each other and, using Bales's (1950) categorisation, the number of 'problem solving attempts' made by contributors. Likeability is also quantified by members rating each other. In addition, the frequency with which other members react to particular contributions is measured.

Perhaps the best known of the group dynamics analysts is Moreno (1953) who developed the sociogram and, whilst maintaining the stance of a quantifier, examined the feelings that existed between members of groups. Not dissimilar to the Bales technique, he used 'positive', 'negative', and 'task orientated' criteria within what was called the 'star-isolate' scale. Principally, this method involves asking group members to evaluate their partners, usually in terms of likeability and trust.

The research design for this investigation included a sub-study using group dynamics techniques to focus upon the question of hierarchy amongst inmate groups. For example, the Bales's scale was used to analyse the interview transcripts from five groups of prisoners. Additionally, respondents were asked to rate one another according to the principles of Moreno's design. This information was most valuable in clarifying the changing roles assumed by inmates during different social episodes.

Prisoners participating in the research

As the focus of this study falls upon persistent young property offenders whose career includes a period of prison department custody, it was decided to conduct the research in a remand and a youth custody centre serving the same geographical region. This arrangement made the research project manageable and contributed towards further understanding of the criminal career. Indeed a number of remand prisoners participating in the study subsequently moved to the youth custody centre chosen for the research. The remand centre was chosen to explore young offenders' first experience of prison custody, although many had previously enjoyed a sojourn in a detention centre. Periods of remand are usually sudden in the sense that the offender is quickly whisked through a series of short steps from the community, sometimes the scene of the crime, to the prison. Detention centre is, as the euphemism suggests, a short, sharp shock.

In order to trace retrospectively the careers of young people remanded to custody or sentenced to youth custody, data were collected from all prison files available on the first day of three periods of fieldwork. The only exclusions were those young people whose records were, for administrative reasons, unavailable. This analysis offers evidence on the background characteristics and career patterns of 186 young people in custody, findings which are presented in Chapter Five.

The qualitative research data was then collected from a group of 45 prisoners aged between 15 and 17 years, randomly selected from the original 186. It was possible to re-interview these 45 inmates in small groups and analyse these transcripts using the group dynamics techniques described above. In order to clarify issues arising from the initial investigation a second stage of interviews, usually more structured and focused, was completed. Finally, five prison officers were interviewed to gather additional perspectives on the experience of life in a prison for young people.

Conclusions

As shall be seen, there are significant gaps in our knowledge about the life of a young offender placed in or sentenced to custody. For example, little is known about the immediate effects of custody, shared rules to guide or govern behaviour or the young offender's view of his offence. Thus, the last two chapters have been concerned with fashioning a method and research design which will produce fresh data relevant to some of these lacunae. In Chapter Two, a framework for understanding young peoples' interpretation of their lifestyle was outlined and rules of behaviour stressed. In this chapter, a range of methods, interviewing, file analysis, non-participant observation and techniques to study group dynamics has been described. From this research design new light is shed upon the young offenders' world.

Summary Points

1. There are many practical and political constraints when conducting research in closed institutions. This study has been vetted but is not sponsored by the Home Office and takes an independent stance.
2. Most institutions harbour a wealth of data in files which provide reliable information on previous offending patterns, movement between institutions and

court disposals for young offenders. These data have been used to map criminal careers.

3. The principal component of the research design is a series of interviews which reveal data about the prisoner's life outside the institution as well as his life inside. A good deal of time has been spent establishing an independent role to encourage openness and confidence amongst interviewees. In order to discover distortion and exaggeration, interviews are conducted individually and then in groups of five.

4. The societal, formal, interaction and belief rules which form the basis of this study have been identified from the transcripts of interviews with inmates. These transcripts were first categorized into the four episodes of the criminal career.

5. Participant observation is impossible in the prison setting but many of its principles and aims can be utilised through non-participant observation, where the group under scrutiny is aware of the researcher's role. Over time, the researcher establishes a rapport with the inmates of the institution under study and groups feel at ease when revealing evidence.

6. There are psychological methods for measuring the dynamics of action which measure and interpret utterances made in conversation within a group. These methods have been used in a sub-study of the hierarchy amongst inmates.

4. The criminal career and the criminal identity

In this chapter, it becomes clear that commitment to a criminal career is facilitated by standard processes of adolescent development and the offender's ability to re-define his predicament. Persistent delinquency reflects the excitement and emotion which crime generates among a reference group. Prisoner's adaptations to security are scrutinized. Early studies of prison as a miniature society stress the continuity of the prison, whilst recent research notes growing unrest and conflict within them. It is suggested that a model which accounts for a variety of adaptations by inmates would be profitable.

Relatively few careers begin at the bottom of the social ladder and end at the top. There are many variations and some social groups are downwardly mobile. For example, Cressey (1932) studied 'Taxi-dancers', women hired by men requiring partners for the dance floor. New entrants to this profession, young and attractive, drew the best customers and earned well. However, as age and hard work dulled the appeal of hirer and hired, so social standing declined and, indeed, many Taxi-dancers subsequently became prostitutes. Commitment to careers that end badly is quite common.

There are many examples of young people selecting a particular lifestyle despite massive cultural pressures to the contrary. Elkind (1979) describes homosexuality as a conscious and courageous choice. For Becker and Strauss (1956), the first step is the most important in commissioning a new career. Becker (1963) notes that the most important component of a non-conformist career is the initial deviance. Most people, he says, experience delinquent impulses, if only in fantasy form, but few transform them into action.

Do individuals make conscious decisions to break the law? Tutt (1973), who views delinquency as a combination of psychological and sociological attributes, notes that achievement motivation, defined as competition to a standard of excellence, is lacking in delinquents. Recently, however, a group of criminologists have applied economic theories to offending behaviour and see crime as the outcome of criminals' choices between options, however hasty or precipitate. For example, Becker (1968) examines the cost-benefit of individual decisions to offend and Clarke (1987) links the economic gains of crime with other expressive goals. As later chapters reveal, although the young people under scrutiny end up in prison, many consider that crime does pay.

Research evidence suggests that individuals intentionally pursue particular career avenues, but it is a mistake to assume a clear life-plan with clear patterns of motivation. Roberts (1974) notes the propensity to drift into jobs which reflect original aims. Often, individuals plump for second choice, prospective doctors become nurses, would-be physicists settle for teaching and as Stewart, Prendy and Blackburn (1980) found, the initial doubts of new recruits soon disappear in a surge of enthusiasm. Thus, decisions regarding career may lead to unintended outcomes but individuals accentuate the advantages of their choice. As will be seen, these are also features of delinquent careers.

The phrase 'career choice' conjures up a picture of the individual distinguishing between a number of alternatives rather as a batsman selects a gap in the field to drive the cricket ball. In reality, there are limited options which change over time. Moreover, choices are seldom immediately apparent and accidents are quite common in successful careers. Indeed, many cricketing centuries have begun with a wild slog of the ball which luckily clears the boundary. Thus, when it is said that young people choose a criminal career, the choice may have more to do with luck than judgement.

Becker (1963) has looked at the various stages in the careers of deviant groups. Initially, deviants adopt a self-justifying rationale or ideology. During the second stage, they acquire the knowledge to conduct their deviance with the minimum of fuss until, finally, they become confident enough to condemn any laws they break. Thus, marijuana users learn how to smoke the drug, recognize the effects and privately enjoy the sensation. Seasoned pot-smokers call for the abolition of certain drug laws using self-justifying rationales, such as marijuana has the same intoxicating effect as alcohol. It will be seen that persistent property offenders similarly become more confident and self-assured about their behaviour over time.

It can, therefore, be seen that there is considerable evidence which suggests that the lifestyle of the young people under scrutiny in this book can be understood as a criminal career. Additionally, there is limited support for some of the theoretical propositions outlined in the opening chapter. Firstly, career choice is a rational decision even when the outcome is different from that originally intended. Secondly, a commitment to careers that end badly, a feature of the persistent property offenders discussed in this study, is not uncommon. Thirdly, the influences of others who share the career route is clear, particularly for deviant groups. However, a number of questions remain. To begin with, there is a need further to explore any incongruity between identity and behaviour in individual careers. Secondly, although some writers identify distinct stages in social careers, few show how the identity changes and develops. Thirdly, although the first step on the career route is found to be the most important, more evidence is needed to show why individuals persist in the absence of tangible rewards and in the face of positive discouragement. Further consideration of the development of a criminal identity may help to answer these questions.

The development of a criminal identity

Any identity will reflect the influences of others in an individual's social networks. Gurin and Townsend (1986) find that members of a group can assume a common fate, for instance we think what happens to our colleagues will affect ourselves. Tajfel (1986) notes that the group's influence can be complex, reflecting perceived dissimilarities as well as similarities between individuals. Many writers have developed theories which build upon the idea that adolescents have relatively long periods of free time during which they help each other to develop an identity independent of family and other adult social ties. On the threshold of adulthood, we come to terms with and understand sexual motivation and learn how to cope with adults (Argyle 1969). During this period, adolescents cultivate consistency in their personality, but are in the happy position of having reduced responsibility for decisions or actions (Lecky 1945, Brown 1965). The development of an 'identity' is a normal part of adolescence; it will be seen that the development of a criminal identity is simply another manifestation of this norm.

These patterns of development are reflected in the sociometric structure of adolescent groups (Sherif and Sherif 1964, Schmuck and Lohman 1965). Adolescents share intense friendships formed within small congregations of three to six which perform few important tasks. Additionally, young people are reticent to evaluate the actions of peers and social expectations tend to be restricted to interpersonal matters as opposed to wider structural demands. As a consequence, hierarchy is noticeably absent. Clearly, as it was proposed at the beginning of this study, shared guidelines and groups of sympathetic followers are important in adolescent development.

Inhelder and Piaget (1958) find that the salient characteristic of the adolescent personality is the ability to deal in potentialities or possibilities. Their research shows that children aged eight years and under are subject to heteronomous morality, they respect adult rules and the expectations of others. As children become older, they begin to construct rules which reflect the needs of their own age group and assume an autonomous morality. It is clear that young people in small groups can distinguish between 'right' and 'wrong' but that their cognitive development increasingly allows them to choose 'wrong' without compunction. How is this possible?

Delinquent action, say Sutherland and Cressey (1970), is possible only if the participant is socialised into a particular system of law-breaking values. These ethics, if learnt, allow individuals to put to one side the great mass of information encouraging law-abiding behaviour. As such, Sutherland and Cressey find that crime seldom begins as a solitary activity, rather it is initiated by groups using codes which supersede those of the dominant culture. This is not to say that a lawless mini-society is created, only that members sometimes choose local codes in preference to state laws. What are these codes?

Matza and Sykes (1957) find that delinquents cancel out the disapproval that the wider society has for criminal activity. This is demonstrated in the analysis of specific utterances given by young offenders in conversation. For example, 'I didn't mean it' is translated as denial of responsibility, and 'I didn't mean to hurt him' is a re-interpretation of injury. Other examples include, 'He was only some queer' (denial of victim); 'Everyone picks on us' (condemning the condemners); and, 'You've got to help your mates' (appeals to higher loyalties). This research scrutinises the meaning particular acts hold for young offenders and emphasises what are called 'techniques of neutralisation' which allow the offender temporarily to become delinquent; to take a 'moral holiday'. As shall be seen later in this study, the ability of young offenders to re-interpret their situation can be key in the development of a criminal identity.

Findings about the delinquent identity offer much support for the theoretical perspectives outlined in the opening chapter. Studies in this area again emphasise the importance of individual choice and shared guidelines in the development of identity and a moral framework. The preceding pages also suggest that a young person's identity can be incongruous with the behaviour pattern and, as Matza has shown, there can be wholesale re-interpretation of particular actions in order to make them seem acceptable. Perspectives on how the identity may develop throughout the career are also apparent and, for example, there are clear and subtle changes in the moral judgement of adolescents, it is not just a case of being good or bad. Moreover, the ability to negate societal disdain and view delinquency in a positive light may lead to an explanation of the persistence in the behaviour of the young people under scrutiny in this study. However, more evidence is required on this issue.

Shared guidelines

So much for ideas about a developing criminal identity and a criminal career. What of the existence of shared guidelines, another proposition explored in this study? Do young property offenders whose criminal behaviour leads to a spell in prison really make use of guidelines developed and maintained by each other? Is there much evidence to suggest that delinquency is a group activity?

In the tradition of American sociology, a number of British studies have focused upon the gang activity of young people. However, apart from Patrick's (1973) work in Glasgow, there is little evidence that gangs in the United Kingdom have any influence upon the criminal career. The studies from the Centre for Contemporary Cultural Studies in Birmingham have produced ethnographies of youth culture in England, but none propose the existence of well organised gang structure. The evidence would suggest that it is rare for a gang's life-span to be longer than one generation of members. Studies in this country of large delinquent assemblies, such as the football hooligans described by Marsh (1978b), reveals their temporary nature and it is unlikely that Patrick's (1973) gangs in Glasgow still exist today.

Humphries (1981), looking at working class culture at the turn of the Century, identified the 'Bengal Tigers', of Manchester, and the 'Peaky Binders', of Birmingham. But these groups largely consisted of unemployed young men who enjoyed tenuous links with professional criminals and, therefore, had access to an alternative social career. Using oral histories, Humphries found that the lower tier gangs were, in fact, very loosely co-ordinated and informal. Indeed, he describes them as 'cliques' with 'no clearly defined status, hierarchy or leadership'.

What the gang offered was a focal point where many of the values of conventional society could be turned upside down. Here, a 'gang' is not a consistent group of people, but a term to describe a setting into which young men drift, where certain common factors, such as tough individualism, immediate excitement and material gain can be exercised. Of course, such a forum can be class-conscious and result, for example, in racist attacks or assaults on the police, but for the most part it is harmless.

The loose organisation and lack of cohesion among English working class boys is evident in Cohen's (1972) case study of the behaviour of Mods and Rockers during the sixties and, in particular, their fights in the holiday resorts of sunny England. Cohen questions the oft-portrayed image of a homogeneous working class. He notes that the young people assembled on the beaches could be described as a series of interlocking crowds rather than a group. Moreover, the young people milled around aimlessly waiting to be entertained. Indeed, Shibutani (1955) has shown excitement to be a collective experience which, for adolescents, is often 'manufactured'.

It would seem that, on the face of it, English youth groups have little co-ordination. However, their behaviour patterns are not anarchic and social scientists have uncovered an underlying structure. For example, Cohen graphically describes the crowd's use of what Shibutani (1966) has called a 'rumours sequence'. This technique roused the assembled groups and created an event which excited not only the participants but also the media. There are four types of rumour used at different times during the period leading up to the disturbance, including; murmurs of unrest before the event; specifically threatening rumours about what might happen; the spark which precipitates the event; and fantastic rumours during and after the event to justify the disturbance.

Cohen effectively describes shared guidelines for group behaviour. As will be seen, the way in which groups of adolescents create excitement from apparently mundane situations is a feature of the early episodes of criminal careers when, for example, burglary is explained as a response to the absence of anything better to do. We should not underestimate the amount of adrenalin produced by a group of bored delinquent boys who turn to housebreaking for distraction.

Are there any other examples of shared guidelines? Marsh (eg. 1978), studying groups of football hooligans who frequented the terraces of the 'Manor Ground' Oxford and the 'Den' at Millwall, explains continuity in behaviour through the group structures that help to co-ordinate hooliganism. The youngest members of the group are the novices, 'little kids' who stand at the bottom of the terrace and spend as much time watching other fans as they do the football. In the middle of the terrace are the rowdies including the aggro leaders who organise surges into opposing fans' territory in such a way that only the inexperienced are hurt and chant leaders who co-ordinate the singing and staccato hand-clapping. There are other roles, for instance, fighter, heavy drinker, hooligan and organiser. There are even social isolates, for example, nutters who can be indiscriminately violent and generally indulge in actions described by other fans as 'out of order'.

Marsh describes a role system in preference to a linear hierarchy including, for instance, leader and follower. The structure, together with the shared guidelines about acceptable behaviour, helps to organise the event in such a way that excitement and aggravation are maximised while physical violence is minimised. Although the terrace may attract different people from one week to the next, from one season to another, behaviour patterns remain the same.

Shared guidelines can also explain continuity in behaviour throughout a career which spans different institutions, for example, school and work. Willis (1977) describes how a loose affiliation of troublesome school boys form a culture which runs parallel to that in the factory. Indeed, these school boys choose a career of tedium and boredom on the shop floor which reflects their experience in school. Furthermore, the strategies learned in school to deal with boredom, blocked opportunities, alienation and lack of control over their own destiny serve the young people well after they have made their 'voluntary choice' to enter the factory. Willis finds continuity between school and factory, the school's response to the actions of particular children helps to propel them to and prepare them for the factory floor. As later chapters in this study reveal, similar continuities are apparent in the criminal career and similar messages about the behaviour of a young person are conveyed by different parts of the juvenile justice system.

Does this evidence on group activity help to explain persistence in delinquent behaviour, a notable lacuna in research evidence on standard adolescent development? Initially, the findings of studies of sub-cultures have not been very helpful; gangs do not lead the innocent to the guilty, nor do they stop the sinner from reforming. It has been shown that, although larger assemblies such as football hooligans or mods and rockers on holiday beaches occasionally gather, gangs differ little from everyday adolescent groups. In a sense, young people use the gang as a reference point where activity or subjects of conversation go beyond those tolerated in small adolescent groups. It will enjoy many different inputs including the criminal and the delinquent. The reference group may partake in a number of activities with, as Argyle (1969) has observed, different leaders for the different activities of the group.

These findings suggest that further exploration of the dynamics of groups of adolescents will be of great value in making assessments of the shared guidelines developed and used by the young people scrutinized in this study. Furthermore, the emotion and excitement delinquency generates among such reference groups will prove a fruitful line of enquiry in the coming pages. It is clear from this evidence that the identity adopted by adolescents may not coincide with the behaviour and, just as football hooligans come together at weekly intervals to create a veneer of violence, in the same way, property offenders may benefit in ways other than material gain. Moreover, further scrutiny may reveal continuity between the different episodes of the criminal career and just as Willis's school boys are learning to labour, the custodial experience may give young offenders an opportunity to study stealing. The criminal identity may well be important in maintaining continuity in the career.

Prisoner adaptation

In this chapter, ideas about the criminal identity, the criminal career and shared guidelines have been explored, these all being central to the theoretical proposition put forward at the beginning of the book. But this study is about young people whose behaviour leads to custody and the continued use of shared guidelines and the maintenance of a criminal identity will depend much on their ability to adapt to prison. These institutions will be trying to deter the inmate from further crime on leaving, but if the prisoner becomes used to his environment, further periods of incarceration may be counter-productive in that they will be subsumed into the criminal identity. Is this a feasible proposition?

As Goffman (1961) notes, the effect on the inmate of a placement in a residential setting is wide-ranging. Concerned to develop a Weberian 'ideal type' total institution, Goffman finds a number of characteristics are common to such places. Firstly, they provide an unusual living setting where there is no personal choice and companions are given rather than sought. This is known as 'batch living'. Secondly, total institutions are marked by the fact that they have two groups of people, the managers and the managed, the staff and the inmates. The relationship between these two groups of people is completely governed by their different status. This is referred to as 'binary management'. Thirdly, those entering a total institution as inmates will be subjected to the gradual process of 'role stripping', where individual habits and foibles are suppressed. Ultimately the long-term inmate becomes a cipher and adopts what Goffman terms the 'inmate role'.

No institution is, in fact, completely open or closed and most, including remand and youth custody centres in England and Wales, have regular transactions with the outside world. However, it will be seen that prison severs the inmate's links with the wider society, restricts his focus to the activity of other inmates and so encourages a criminal career.

The wider effects of prison on the inmate are, of course, considerable. Sykes (1958) describes the 'pains of imprisonment', including loss of liberty, the lack of goods and services, the deprivation of heterosexual relationships and the loss of both autonomy and security. As he notes, 'the worst thing about being a prisoner is that you have to live with other prisoners'.

However, a number of factors collude to lessen the impact of prison upon the lives of young offenders and thus contribute to continuities in institutional life. There is a great deal of evidence, mostly arising from scrutiny of adult prisons, which suggests that the inmate leads a conflict-free life and creates structures which allow him to relax and learn. In this model, prisoners live in relative harmony with each other. Indeed, Hood and Sparks (1970) suggest that prisoners 'move in a direction of solidarity' in order to avoid the problems consequent upon life in a closed setting. The prisoner, for Hood and Sparks, is in search of an easy, concordant prison experience, doing his 'bird' as gracefully as possible.

Gordon Rose (1956, 1956b and 1959), who focused upon patterns of interaction in a borstal, proposes that borstal boys assume set roles which help organise institutional life. There are leaders, their followers and aides who all set a bad example to other inmates. On the other hand, there are social isolates including independent and rejected residents. Rose describes a clear hierarchical structure with set roles for the participants, an image mirrored in pictures of prison life provided by the mass media, for instance Alan Clarke's film *Scum*.

Much of the literature concerned with adult prisons has presented the institution as a miniature society, facets of which mirror the outside world. In one of the earliest pieces of research to use this approach Schrag (1954) shows that prisoners develop their own language and create sub-divisions within the system. Each inmate is categorised by the others and each category gives an indication of the role and status taken by members of the group. Schrag cites five; (1) Right guys (anti-social); (2) Square johns (pro-social); (3) Politicians (pseudo-social); (4) Outlaws (asocial); and (5) Dings (unstable, unpredictable). Similar work by Sykes (1958) discusses the inmate code which, he claimed, was developed and used by prisoners as a part of the system in which they lived.

Although it is doubtful that empirical findings from the United States about adults will transfer wholesale to this study which applies to young people in England and Wales, those studies on prisoners' code and role systems are most useful in developing the propositions outlined in the opening chapter. The use of shared guidelines would appear to be a common feature of institutional life. Moreover, this evidence helps to explain the continuity in a behaviour pattern when the rewards are so bleak. For if incarceration reduces life chances but the custodial experience includes supports and camaraderie from other inmates, why should the prisoner see repeated spells of custody as a poor option? Indeed, it is possible to see why offenders persist with a criminal identity when the pains of imprisonment are sharp. Hood, Sparks and Sykes describe a society with clear roles, expectations and codes of good conduct for inmates; observance of these norms allow prisoners to enjoy a relatively conflict-free world. This cohesive structure helps to compensate for the less enjoyable aspects of prison life. However, in this model, there is little room for antagonisms that must exist when groups of males are placed together. Indeed, this omission has led to sustained criticism from those whose research reveals unease and discord within our prisons.

Later evidence, for example Cline and Wheeler (1968), notes the way in which prisoners react to the rituals of institutional life. These studies have quite a different slant. Gone is the routine which makes for harmony in prison. This is replaced by turmoil and an inmate's behaviour is interpreted as a reaction to his predicament. Gone is the placid prisoner. In the new model the incarcerated seek to create a life from their unpromising surroundings. Gone is the acquiescent prison officer, who is now referred to as guard and becomes keeper or oppressor.

This change of emphasis may be related to the time in which the studies took place. Early investigations were conducted when prisons were stable and safe communities, ideal settings for the sociologist anxious to test out new theories on human guinea-pigs, who were, literally, captive. Recent studies have taken place in an atmosphere of relative unease. There have been a number of quite serious riots and conflicts between prison administrators, prisoners and prison officers. The conditions in which the inmate is kept have slowly deteriorated over the last two decades, so that today's prisoner suffers more than mere deprivation of liberty and prison officers remain unhappy with their working conditions. The pains of imprisonment have intensified.

At the same time, research has questioned prisoner solidarity. For example, prisoner codes may be anything but definite and/or unchanging (Hood and Sparks, 1970). Further, evidence suggests that prisoners are apt to pay mere lip service to codes of conduct. Dunlop and McCabe (1965), Clarke and Martin (1971) and Polsky (1962) have all noted the fluctuating character of residential centres for young people as inmates leave and arrive, data which has been duplicated in adult prisons by King and Elliot (1977). Cline and Wheeler (1968) rehearse these arguments during scrutiny of fifteen penal institutions in Scandinavia. Using three hypothetical examples of behaviour which indicated opposition to staff and the official rules of the institution, they found that inmate codes are also responsible for much anti-social behaviour and vary with the geographical background of the inmates.

Recent autobiographies by prisoners also reveal conflict. John McVicar (1974) may have shared similar values with Wally Probyn (1977) during their stay in Durham maximum security wing but neither is very complimentary about another well known criminal of the time, John Richardson. In a similar vein, Jimmy Boyle (1977) found fellow inmates practically impossible to live with until he was eased into the therapeutic community in Barlinie maximum security prison. It is clear that, although prisoners may use shared guidelines in everyday life, the prescriptions may lead to anti-social behaviour and disharmony in a controlled environment.

It can be seen that there is a dearth of research material from the United Kingdom on young people in prison. Nonetheless, certain things about the criminal identity adopted by persistent young property offenders whose career includes prison custody are revealed by the analysis just considered. It can be seen how shared guidelines are important to institutional life and may help to shape a criminal identity. However, whilst a group of inmates may together ameliorate the pains of imprisonment, there are also findings which suggest that when groups of young men are placed together in a closed setting, conflict will ensue.

The research evidence from the remand and the youth custody centre study will clarify particular aspects of the criminal identity of the young offenders when they are incarcerated. The findings explore individual adaptation, how the identity changes between the episodes under scrutiny and the importance of particular events in shaping the identity. Moreover, with this data it is possible to examine how conflict amongst prisoners and between prisoners and prison officers is channelled.

The evidence collected for this book shows that it is a mixture of conflict and harmony within a prison setting that allows it to function. For example, the pains of imprisonment press more heavily on some prisoners than others. Relative tranquillity and harmony within institutions can be relieved by explosions of conflict and aggression. There may be apparent harmony between prisoners and prison officers but individual events such as the challenging of prison laws are likely to crystalise the uneven balance of power between the two parties. Let us look more carefully at the importance of individual adaptations in the prisoner's choice of identity.

Prisoner choices

How do prisoners choose between styles of adaptation and particular patterns of interaction? Dunlop and McCabe (1965) found that soon after their arrival and their first experience of the 'short, sharp, shock', young men in detention centres were subdued, apprehensive and mistrustful of the prison regime. On leaving, however, the inmates placed far more importance on the influence of the delinquent groups and expressed resentment of the general loss of liberty they had suffered as opposed to individual items in the daily routine. Wheeler (1961), scrutinising relationships between prisoner and prison officer, found that during the first months of their sentence, when prisoners are finding their way, they are very conformist. This pattern of behaviour is repeated during the last few months of sentence when there are expectations of and hopes for parole or remission. However, in the intervening period, the inmate plays the system and is subject to bouts of non-conformity.

Clemmer (1958) proposes that male prisoners develop through a linear process of socialisation of three stages. In stage one, the inmate accepts an inferior role in relation to his peers. In the second stage, he accumulates new facts which tend to compound rather than negate his new found status. Finally, the prisoner develops novel habits which, before sentence, were anathema. It is during this, the third stage, that the prisoner becomes happy within himself and full re-adjustment in role and status is possible. These studies provide valuable back-up to the proposition that the identity of those under scrutiny will change at different points in the criminal career.

Further evidence of the changing ambience of a prison wing emerges from King and Elliot's (1977) study of Albany, before it became a high security dispersal prison. Using a framework developed by Irwin (1970), this study discovered a variety of responses by prisoners to their predicament including 'jailing' (involvement with sub-culture and, for example, dealing in contraband) and gleaning (frequent contact with specialist treatment staff). It is clear from this evidence that inmates exercise choice in assuming roles and behaviour patterns.

Cohen and Taylor's (1981) study of Durham prison stresses the importance of banal, everyday issues. Particular emphasis is put upon prisoners' ability to create an interesting environment from the minimum of resources, a contribution which helps to maintain the viability of a prison community. The basis for Cohen and Taylor's observation is Berger and Luckman's (1971) work on socialisation and the propensity of individuals to develop conceptual machineries which help cope with the stresses of everyday life. Cohen and

Taylor note that in prison, the ability to cope reflects social skills which can re-vitalise those ordinary, mundane issues which assume little significance to those at liberty. Once again, it becomes clear that prisoners choose from limited options and, in an institution, inconsequential issues become a matter of 'life or death'.

Giallombardo (1966), looking at a women's prison known as Alderson, has noted temporary changes in the behaviour of prisoners who are anxious to make their time go a little easier, for example, some inmates took traditional male roles. The Alderson study acknowledges that prisoners' behaviour is quite different from that observed before their arrival in a penal institution and they are unlikely to repeat such patterns of action on release. However, apart from data seen as being essential to this type of study, for example, the offence history of prisoners under scrutiny or, in the case of Alderson, whether inmates were married, had children, et cetera, no attempt is made to understand the contribution of prisoners to the daily life of the institution, to comment upon changes in identity whilst in prison or to speculate on the effect of return for those paroled. Indeed, for many studies, especially those concerned with prison as a miniature society, it is the isolation of the community from outside forces that makes the research so interesting.

In essence, the prison is a community and its roles, codes and emotional tone are likely to change as participants come and go. In studies which can dispense with the need to differentiate between deviants and conformists, variations become more apparent. Bartak and Rutter (1975) assess the impact of different regimes upon the interaction of staff and autistic children in residential care. The data from this study reveal a continually changing scene. For example, they find that staff behaviour is widely divergent, fluctuates with time and has a marked effect upon the institutional ambience. It is noteworthy that prison staff, in comparison, are often described in the penological literature as automatons, although they regain their character in literary, film and television interpretations of prisons. It is possible to conclude that remand and youth custody centres are communities as volatile and difficult to categorise as other informal social settings, making the task of charting the development of the criminal career and identity all the more difficult. As if these problems were not enough, the prison community is only part of a young person's life and is linked to experiences before sentence and expectations on leaving.

There is, however, one study which incorporates the nuances of institutional life and links them into the wider perspective of the child's life. Polsky (1962), observing the 'therapeutic milieu' of a community for emotionally disturbed delinquent boys and girls, notes the common motives for interaction and the way in which different types of social meeting affect different individuals. He shows the way in which there develops a structure with a hierarchy of status and standardised values that informally regulate the activities of gatherings. He shows the mechanisms of social control, violence, scapegoating, ranking and manipulation. Amongst other studies of institutional life for young people, Polsky's is quite different for he identifies constant reproduction of the institutional community. Whilst the informal social system is related to the formal system, the inmates are seen to have far more autonomy and control over their day-to-day lives.

Conclusions

It is clear from the evidence considered in this chapter that career choice can be understood as behaviour which is rational to the individual, even when careers end badly. It is also apparent that the influence of sympathetic others is important to the continuity of careers. Indeed, the identity of the young offender develops in much the same way as others who do not become involved with the police, although the decisions which lead to relatively serious crimes such as burglary have received scant attention in the work of other writers.

The use of shared guidelines to behaviour, developed and maintained by groups of young people, have been noted, particularly in prison where the inmates adapt in order to overcome the pains of imprisonment. Throughout this chapter, the ability of young people to reinterpret their predicament has been highlighted; the victims are disparaged, 'he was only some queer' say Matza's delinquents, 'I'll do my bird, no problems', say the prisoners interviewed for this study. Thus, the state's response to continued delinquency is subsumed into the identity and the juvenile justice system, rather than deterring further criminal activity, contributes to the continuance of the career.

Summary Points

1. Crime can be understood as a career choice which is rational. Early decisions and accidents help open new routes, but commitment to careers that end badly is not uncommon.
2. Adolescence is an extremely important time of life which sees amongst other things, the development of moral conceptions and ego-identity. Adolescents form groups consisting of three to six others. It is a time of experimentation and usually involves some delinquency.

3. Evidence from studies focusing on young people's interpretation of delinquency shows that adolescents tend to take moral holidays, that they drift in and out of crime following the neutralization of societal laws. Often, delinquency is only temporary.
4. Gangs or groups of possibly criminal and delinquent young people have existed, in some form or other, for some time, but their activities are often exaggerated. One realistic possibility is that the gang is no more than a reference group which serves different functions for a number of youngsters. It is suggested that a young offender's persistence with crime is not the result of participation in a large gang, but the excitement and emotion the activity generates among the tolerant reference group.
5. Total institutions are characterised by batch living, binary management and role stripping. There is little empirical evidence to compare remand and youth custody centres with the total institution model and assess the impact upon the criminal career.
6. There is evidence of relative tranquillity within prisons, particularly from studies which view the institution as a miniature society isolated from the outside world it mirrors. Code and role systems make for a conflict-free life for the prisoners and prison officers. Other evidence stresses prisoners' reaction to rituals. Such a view has been viewed as a response to the changing nature of prison. In this model prisoners are in solidarity against the prison officer and prisoners are said to pay lip service to code and role systems.
7. It will be more realistic to consider the institution as a place where conflicts have to be managed. Moreover, the ambience of any institution is likely to reflect the situation of its current residents.
8. Choice within a prison is limited and mundane issues become very important in the daily life of a prisoner.

5. Who goes to prison?

In this chapter data drawn from prison records and official statistics are considered. It is found that entry to prison for young burglars and car thieves is rare. The characteristics of residents and career patterns consequent to court disposals are scrutinized.

The following chapters trace the careers of young offenders destined for prison custody. Initially, the files of 186 inmates in the remand and youth custody centre were scrutinized. Selected randomly from this group, 45 young people were then interviewed at length and participated in other parts of the study, for example the study of the dynamics of prisoner groups.

This chapter offers findings from the files of the 186 inmates supplemented by findings from other research and government statistics. The characteristics of the young people and special features about their career routes are described. Focus falls upon the age and geographical background of the inmates. Further, their court careers and involvement with agencies of welfare and control are traced. The number of prison placements experienced by prisoners as part of one sentence and, of course, their offence histories are laid out.

Let us begin by looking at the proportion of offences which result in a young 14-17 year old male being remanded in custody or sentenced to youth custody.

How many get into custody?

As a society, we do not lightly send young people to prison. Penal policy in the twentieth century has been concerned to develop a justice system which distinguishes juvenile from adult criminals and efforts to divert young offenders away from prison department establishments are now more rigorous. Indeed, it is now most difficult for a burglar or car thief successfully to pursue a career which takes in remand and youth custody centres. Nonetheless, in recent years custodial regimes for young people have become harsher and the numbers of people sentenced to prison department detention has markedly increased. How do these apparently contradictory statements fit together?

The past twenty years have witnessed two pieces of legislation, one which threatened major developments in the use of custody for young people and one which has accomplished significant changes. The 1969 Children and Young Persons Act attempted to wrest power away from the magistrates by allowing more of the decisions about the disposal of guilty offenders to be taken by other welfare agencies. Had it been fully implemented, the 1969 Act would have raised the age of criminal responsibility from 10 to 14 and abolished sentences to detention and youth custody centre for young people aged less than 17 years. Although it allowed significant advances in other areas, the 1969 legislation did little to reduce the number of young people sentenced to custody.

The 1982 Criminal Justice Act on the other hand, has precipitated a rise in the use of penal incarceration for young offenders in England and Wales. The 1982 Act had the effect of returning the power taken from magistrates following the implementation of the 1969 legislation. Magistrates now have increased powers to sentence young people to detention centres, for a shorter minimum of 21 days, or to a determinate sentence of youth custody which replaced borstals but operated from the same institutions. Since the implementation of the 1982 Criminal Justice Act, magistrates can sentence 15 to 16 year olds to youth custody for periods ranging between four and twelve months.

The contrast in the changing aims of juvenile justice reflected by these two pieces of legislation is aptly summed up by Stewart and Tutt (1987) when they say,

> Borstal and detention centres were, under the 1969 Act, initially to be phased out and yet over the decade showed a massive increase in use of over 200 per cent. For detention centres figures rose from 2,016 in 1971 to 5,412 in 1981; for borstal (both boys and girls), the numbers rose from 1,116 in 1971 to 2,382 in 1981. Thus, these ten years saw a major growth in the use of security and custody for all types for young people. The implementation of the Criminal Justice Act 1982 has had a mixed effect on this growth. Early indications are that the use of detention centres for under 17 years is dropping (-15 per cent), whereas youth custody is increasing (+69 per cent).

However, despite these increased numbers, delinquent adolescents are not lightly sentenced to custody and most who are detained experience a variety of avenues through the juvenile justice system, each of which leads to contact with different agencies of welfare and control. Initially, a young offender of 16 must have his crime reported to the police who then must apprehend the offender and decide to deal with the case in a formal rather than an informal manner. Often, where the offence is minor, a police officer will deal with the misdemeanour informally, for example, by way of a stern warning or with a formal caution at the police station, often in the presence of parents. In other cases, the police may decide to take no further action.

As the following table illustrates, if a magistrate or judge is called upon to pass judgement, a tariff of punishment is available including several alternatives to custody. In 1987 just under one half (49.6%) of young people aged 14 to 21 years of age had their offence summarily disposed of by way of an absolute discharge or fine. Additionally, a range of community-based options are available to the court. It can place a young person under a supervision order, where the supervisor is a probation officer or social worker. The court can also impose specific activities to accompany the order and often this involves an intermediate treatment agency. Young people can be made to spend free time at an attendance centre. They can be asked to help others in the community by way of a community service order. They can be supervised at home by a probation officer under a probation order. Alternatively, he or she can be committed to the care of the local authority. This option may bring into operation a wide range of services, some of which will be residential, while other young offenders may be fostered or allowed to live at home under supervision. Just under a third (30.8%) of offenders aged between 14 and 21 years of age received a community based sentence in 1987, a proportion which has increased significantly since 1980 (23.9%).

Approximately one fifth (18.3%) of male young offenders coming before the courts are, however, being sent to some form of prison department establishment. Just under one-third of those receiving a custodial sentence are despatched to a detention centre. Stays in these institutions are short and have in recent years become very brief indeed, for as little as three weeks in duration. A second custodial option currently available to the courts for the young offender aged 15 to 21 years is youth custody. These institutions shelter young offenders who might have received a prison sentence had they been adult. Since they have been re-named youth custody centres, sentences have been shortened, the occupational and educational training facilities reduced and the institutional regimes considerably toughened. Nonetheless, maximum security is not always essential and nine of the 22 centres for young men operate relatively open conditions.

Table 5.1: Disposals of males aged 14-21 years in 1980 and 1987

Disposal	1980 %	1987 %
Discharges	11.0	13.9
Fine	45.5	35.7
Supervision Order	6.1	4.7
Attendance Centre	5.7	5.6
Care Order	1.4	0.4
Probation Order	5.0	8.9
Community Service	5.7	11.2
Detention Centre	7.0	5.4
Borstal/Youth Custody	4.8	12.9
Prison	3.9	-
Suspended sentence	2.7	-
Other	1.2	1.2
	100.0	100.0
Summary Tariff	56.5	49.6
Community Based	23.9	30.8
Custodial Sentence	15.7	18.3
Other	3.9	1.2
	100.0	99.9
	(N=169,400)	(N=134,100)

Source: Criminal Statistics England and Wales, 1981 and 1988

It can therefore be seen that recent changes in policy have resulted in an increase in both the proportion of young people sentenced to custody and those required to fulfil orders of the court in the community. However, a very different perspective is arrived at if we consider how many burglaries result in a young person being remanded or sentenced to custody.

The following exercise provides an estimate of how many burglaries result in a young offender being remanded to custody or sentenced to youth custody. It has been necessary to assume that each burglary is committed by a lone offender and that each burglar has an equal chance of pursuing the various avenues of the juvenile justice system. These are false assumptions. As later chapter will show, many burglaries are group events and the experienced delinquent will be treated less leniently than a novice. Nonetheless, it is felt that the exercise provides a good estimate based upon available statistics and it does reveal how difficult it is for the property offender to be sent to prison.

Initially, any house-breaker has at least a one-in-two chance of escaping detection for only a half of all burglaries are notified to the police (Home Office 1982, 1983). For a variety of reasons, many victims of burglary do not feel that the offence warrants police intervention (Radzinowicz and King 1977). Even when the police know of a crime, they are not always successful in clearing it up. Indeed, less than a third of burglaries investigated by a constabulary result in an offender being charged (Home Office 1988). Thus, as the following table shows, for every 1,000 burglaries in England and Wales it is estimated that only 150 offenders will be charged with the offence.

The vast majority (96%) of burglars prosecuted or cautioned by the police are male and a significant proportion (54%) are aged between 14 and 21 years. As has been seen, not all offenders are prosecuted by the police. A small proportion (21%) of males aged 14 to 21 years, arrested for and admitting to burglary are cautioned (Home Office 1988), others will have no further action taken against them. Indeed, it is calculated that for every 1,000 burglaries in England and Wales only 64 young males will be found guilty by a magistrates' or crown court. Again, these statistics are illustrated in the following table.

It is difficult to estimate the proportion of young burglars who are subsequently remanded in custody to await trial or sentence but the one-quarter of all persons proceeded against for burglary and remanded to custody acts as a rough guide (Home Office 1984b). The criminal statistics are much clearer on sentences to custody and it can be predicted that only eight of the 64 prosecutions in 1988 are sentenced to youth custody. Thus, it is possible to estimate that for every 1,000 burglaries committed in 1988, at the very most twenty-four young males will be experiencing a sojourn in a remand and/or a youth custody centre. The figures for car thieves differ little and so, it can be seen, that the offenders scrutinized in this study account for only a tiny minority of crimes committed.

These findings accord with results from the most extensive evidence on the criminal career assembled by the Cambridge Study in Delinquent Development. This research team followed the lives of 411 young males from their eighth to 25th birthdays and found enduring delinquency to be a rare phenomenon. They found that, although a high proportion of adolescents are delinquent, few become persistently criminal. For example, West and Farrington (1973 and 1977) find that almost a third of London boys will have a criminal record by the age of 21 years but that less than half of this group subsequently appear in court. Thus, as they and others (for example, Robins

1978) have noted, whilst most adult prisoners have been adolescent recidivists, not all adolescent recidivists become adult prisoners.

Table 5.2 An estimated outcome of 1,000 burglaries committed in 1988

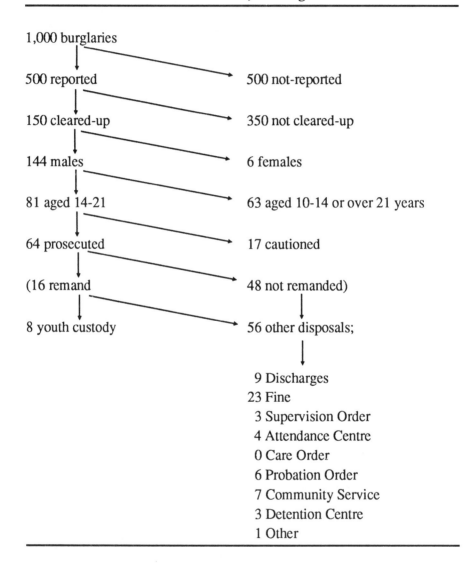

1,000 burglaries

500 reported → 500 not-reported

150 cleared-up → 350 not cleared-up

144 males → 6 females

81 aged 14-21 → 63 aged 10-14 or over 21 years

64 prosecuted → 17 cautioned

(16 remand → 48 not remanded)

8 youth custody → 56 other disposals;

9 Discharges
23 Fine
3 Supervision Order
4 Attendance Centre
0 Care Order
6 Probation Order
7 Community Service
3 Detention Centre
1 Other

Nonetheless, as a society we devote a disproportionate amount of time and resource researching, caring for and locking-up persistent young offenders. Is there anything about the characteristics of this group which makes them stand apart from other youngsters and are there any cogent differences between the remandees and youth custody centre boys?

Characteristics of the residents of remand and youth custody centres

The inmates of youth custody and remand centres form only a small part, in numerical terms, of the work of the prison department of the Home Office. In 1987, the average daily male population of the prison system was just under 49,000. Under a quarter of these young men were living in remand centres (3,322) or youth custody centres (7,803). The numbers passing through these institutions is obviously greater. In 1987, over 15,000 young males experienced youth custody and some 26,000 untried and unsentenced males below the age of 21 were remanded to custody (Home Office 1988, see also King and Morgan 1976).

Of those entering youth custody centres in 1987, only a quarter were below the age of eighteen years, the cut-off point for this study. Nearly two-thirds of all receptions have been sentenced to youth custody because of property offences, for example burglary (39%), theft, handling stolen goods, fraud and forgery (21%). The majority were persistent delinquents, a third (29%) of young people aged 15 or 16 entering youth custody in 1985 have six or more previous convictions and three-quarters (71%) have been found guilty on three or more occasions.

Stewart and Tutt (1987) give detailed information on the previous experience of young people aged under 17 years in custody. One-third of this group had a previous conviction which resulted in custody, one-third had previously been to a detention centre, ten per cent to a youth custody centre. Many of the young people in custody are already well known to the statutory authorities. For example, of Stewart and Tutt's sample, almost a half (48%) had been subject to a care order, 12 per cent had been given a probation order, whilst 47 per cent had enjoyed social services supervision. Over three-quarters of this group had been removed from their families at some stage in the past, although a small but significant group are experiencing separation for the first time when they are sent to prison.

Additional perspectives are available from the characteristics of the residents of the remand and the youth custody centres participating in this study. Initially, it can be seen that young offenders are placed with older, possibly more experienced, prisoners. The following table shows that, of the

186 residents in the two centres coming under scrutiny, only a small majority (57%) had reached their 18th birthday. In the remand centre, the wing under study catered specially for the young and, consequently, the average age of residents was some 21 months less than in the youth custody centre.

The mix of offenders with different ages and offences will be considered further in the coming chapters. It will be remembered that the study group includes a minority -one fifth of the remand centre wing and one tenth of the youth custody centre trainees- aged 14 or 15 years. In the youth custody centre, contact with more experienced offenders was common and nearly two-thirds of residents were aged 18 years and over. In the remand centre, the four inmates who had reached the age of majority were accused or awaiting sentence for serious offences such as murder and rape. They had been placed with younger prisoners for their own protection.

Table 5.3 Age of inmates in the youth custody and remand centre

Age	Youth Custody %	Remand %	All %
14	-	4.2	1.6
15	6.1	15.5	9.7
16	13.0	49.3	26.9
17	19.1	16.9	18.3
18	23.5	8.5	17.7
19	15.7	2.8	10.8
20	16.5	2.8	11.3
21	5.2	-	3.2
22	0.9	-	0.5
	(N=115)	(N=71)	(N=186)
MEAN	18.0 years	16.3 years	17.4 years

As the following table illustrates, not all of the residents of the remand and the youth custody centre wing were well known to the courts. Indeed, nearly one-tenth of the inmates found themselves in custody after one court appearance and another ten per cent had experienced only two disposals. As West and Farrington's (1977) research discovered, in a few isolated cases criminal behaviour first appears as a problem in early adult life. Despite being younger, the remand centre population were better known to the justice system than the youth custody residents, whilst overall, the mean number of court appearances was approaching five.

However, perhaps the most important point to be drawn from this evidence is that neither population had enjoyed a common experience and, for example, although a minority of inmates had only recently been introduced to the courts, others had been down this route as many as 15 times.

Moreover, the inmate with a small number of court appearances is not necessarily an angel temporarily fallen from grace. Indeed, one 16 year old in the study population who was remanded to custody awaiting trial had a number of offences dealt with in one court appearance.

On the 22nd of March, John Smith stole £540 of goods from a clothes shop. Four weeks later he slipped £10 out of a newsagent's till and broke into another shop to realise £460 worth of goods. The following week John temporarily returned to school (at three o'clock in the morning) and stole computer equipment valued at £85. On Mayday, he raided a dry-cleaning firm and escaped with £365 worth of equipment in a stolen Peugeot car. Unhappy with the car's performance, he traded it in for another French model the following day. John Smith was arrested the following week, 200 miles from home, with the booty of the previous night's escapade; £500 worth of video equipment. Despite having no previous convictions, this young man had amassed over £2,000 of stolen goods (not including the two cars) in a period of seven weeks. In the remand centre, he was able to contemplate ten charges of burglary, theft, car theft and numerous minor offences.

Table 5.4 Number of court appearances with a conviction for youth custody and remand centre inmates

Number	Youth Custody %	Remand %	All %
0-2	26.1	18.3	23.1
3-4	27.0	32.4	29.0
5-6	25.2	28.2	26.3
7-8	17.4	16.9	17.2
9-10	3.5	1.4	2.7
11+	0.8	2.8	1.6
	(N=115)	(N=71)	(N=186)
MEAN	4.5	4.8	4.6

John is not representative of the sample population as a whole, the majority of whom were well known to the courts and have had many offences disposed of in the past. However, it is most difficult to find any case which fully describes the variety of experiences enjoyed by the residents of the two prison department establishments under scrutiny.

It is clear that those who were well known to the courts had experienced a range of interventions from relatively straight-forward fines to penal custody, including detention centres. The following table illustrates the proportion of young people in each institution who had enjoyed the differing welfare and control interventions provided for in the justice system in England and Wales.

It is difficult to know whether the numbers in each of the following categories are high or low. For example, would it be expected that more than 57 per cent of the sample group would have been previously fined by the courts? Is it surprising that over half of the prisoners looked at had been to a detention centre in the past but that less than a third were previously subject to a care order? Whatever answer is arrived at, it is surely the case that not all of the disposals available to the courts are exhausted before resorting to prison custody.

The following table also shows that there are statistically significant differences in the type of sentence imposed by the court on remandees and youth custody centre residents. Firstly, significantly more remandees had experienced a period in the care of the local authority than youth custody residents. Secondly, significantly fewer of those on remand had been placed on a community service order. Thirdly, those in youth custody had been given more orders and punishments than their counterparts on remand (mean average 3.8 and 3.2 respectively). However, it is noteworthy that most of the remandees were awaiting or facing a further sentence from the court as part of their current placement.

Patterns arising from court disposals

The following table also shows that over 15 per cent of the prisoners on remand had previously been sent to youth custody. Moreover, the prisoners' records reveal that eight per cent of the youth custody boys were experiencing the placement for the second time. Thus, many of the study population were well versed in the vagaries of custodial care.

Indeed, many of the youth custody residents experienced a number of prison establishments as part of one sentence. One-third (35%) of the 98 inmates, on whom information was available, had been remanded in custody to await their sentence and all had been sent to one, sometimes two or three, local prisons for allocation to an open youth custody centre. In total, these young people experienced 245 placements in prison, an average of 2.5 each, as part of one youth custody sentence. Although the youth custody residents under scrutiny enjoyed an 'open' environment, they will almost certainly have experienced life in more secure and severe settings where conditions are poor and overcrowding common.

Table 5.5 Previous disposals experienced by youth custody and remand centre inmates

Previous Disposals	Youth Custody %	Remand %	All %
Fined	58.3	56.1	57.5
Discharges	44.3	60.6	50.3
Supervision	41.7	45.5	43.1
Care orders	21.7	37.9	27.6
Attendance Centres	31.3	47.0	37.0
Probation	11.3	6.1	9.4
Community Service	15.7	-	9.9
Detention Centre	52.2	56.1	53.6
Youth Custody	100.0	15.2	69.1
	(N=115)	(N=71)	(N=186)
Mean no. of offences	3.77	3.24	3.57

The prisoners' movement through the juvenile justice system has been further explored and analysed by mapping each court disposal over each young person's life on graph paper. Court appearances and their outcomes were arranged in such a fashion that a comparison between different careers and observation of common trends at particular moments in time was possible. A number of points arise from this analysis.

Initially, it is clear that one group of prisoners receives scant attention from the courts and enters the prison system with little preparation or fore-warning. This group may be experienced offenders but it is unlikely they will be familiar with the rudiments of residential care.

This analysis further shows that there is no clear tariff of disposals from the court. It is not uncommon to find that magistrates sentenced a youngster to detention centre after his third appearance for burglary, but then only imposed a fine when he next sat in the dock for exactly the same offence. It is unusual for the courts to repeat a disposal and, for example, two consecutive sentences to youth custody was rare. Thus, if a strong intervention, such as some form of prison custody, is attempted early on in the criminal career, it will most likely be followed by somewhat milder attempts to curb the behaviour pattern.

These data also showed that for those offenders who have long experience of the courts, the pattern of contact is exponential. Early interventions can be relatively successful and a fine or a care order may be followed by many months of apparent inactivity. Later, disposals by the court become less successful and the period between appearances increasingly shorter. Indeed, for most of this group, contact with the agencies of welfare and control becomes a constant feature. Even during periods of liberty from prison, there are fines to pay, care and probation orders to serve and conditions of community service orders to meet. Thus, the young people under study have not ceased their criminal behaviour despite frequent treatment, punishment and threats of further action by the courts.

Table 5.6 The relationship between various types of court disposal during the careers of the study population

	CD etc	SO	CO	AC	PO	CSO	DC	YC
Fines	0.9102	0.2447	0.8790	0.0633	0.3067	*0.0267*	1.0000	0.8484
Discharges		*0.0132*	*0.0078*	*0.0077*	0.9259	0.4008	*0.0044*	0.4066
Supervision Orders			0.3960	*0.0013*	1.0000	0.6325	*0.0035*	0.5102
Care Orders				0.3911	0.5392	0.7114	*0.0018*	0.4590
Attendance Centre					0.3895	0.6113	*0.0208*	0.0722
Probation Orders						0.1104	0.4867	0.5600
Community Service							1.0000	*0.0043*
Detention Centre								0.3005

Figures represent significance level in 2x2 table, figures in italics are significant at $p<0.05$; CD etc=Absolute or Conditional Discharge; SO=Supervision Order; CO=Care Order; AC=Attendance Centre Order; PO=Probation Order; CSO=Community Service Order; DC=Detention Centre; YC=Youth Custody.

The analysis of the previous sentences which had been applied to the study population suggests that there is a statistical relationship between particular types of court disposal. The preceding table, 5.6, lays out the significance level in a two-by-two table for each relationship, whilst table, 5.7 illustrates the statistically significant relationships. They show that a young prisoner who had previously been given a conditional or absolute discharge was also likely to have been placed under a supervision order, although it is not possible to say which disposal came first. For those whose crime results in a period of remand or a sentence to youth custody, certain career routes are more likely than others.

Table 5.7 Significant relationships between various types of court disposal during the careers of the study population

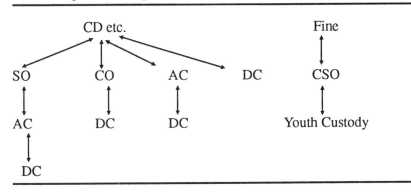

CD etc. = Absolute or Conditional Discharge; DC=Detention Centre; SO=Supervision Order; CO=Care Order; AC=Attendance Centre Order; CSO=Community Service Order

It is more difficult to categorize and analyse the crimes committed by young offenders during their career, especially when prison records are the data source. Official statistics provide a few clues. It is known that over a third of all crime is attributed to males aged between 14 and 21 years. As the following government statistics illustrate, involvement in crime which is known to the police appears to peak during the 14th, 15th and 16th years and decrease thereafter. Thus, Rutter and Giller (1983) are able to remark that 'it is clear that in many cases delinquency proves to be a transient phenomenon with few identifiable sequelae at least in early life.'

Table 5.8 reveals that there seem to be variations in adolescent involvement in different types of crime. For example, the burglary rate for males peaks during the ages 14 to 16 years, whilst the rate of crimes of violence is at its highest for those aged 17 to 21. Similarly, fraud is more likely amongst older adolescents, but theft is more frequent amongst the younger age group.

Such patterns were not apparent in data emerging from remand and youth custody centre records. However, a few noteworthy points arose from the information available and these are illustrated in the following table 5.9.

Table 5.8 Crime rate* amongst males by age and type of crime in England and Wales, 1987

| Age | Type of Offence | | | | | |
	Theft	Burglary	Violence	Fraud	ALL	(N)
10-13	17.2	4.7	1.0	0.2	24.8	(30,300)
14-16	45.1	14.4	6.2	1.0	73.9	(82,300)
17-20	33.0	12.7	9.3	2.5	70.8	(114,100)
21+	5.4	1.3	1.8	0.9	12.8	(221,200)
ALL	10.2	3.0	2.5	1.0	21.8	(447,900)

(Abstracted from Criminal Statistics (Home Office, 1988). *Rate represents those found guilty or cautioned per 1,000 of the population)

Table 5.9 Proportion of prisoners charged or found guilty of different types of criminal offence at some point in their career

Offence	Youth Custody %	Remand %	TOTAL %
Burglary	82.2	84.5	84.9
Car Theft	53.0	50.7	52.2
Violence	11.3	23.9	16.1
Theft	80.9	84.5	82.3
Minor	69.6	69.0	69.4
Fraud	8.7	2.8	6.5
Damage	22.6	23.9	23.1
Sexual	-	4.2	1.6
Other Serious	-	2.8	1.1
	(N=115)	(N=71)	(N=186)

It would seem that the young offenders became involved in crimes from a number of the categories listed. The most frequent crimes committed by the remand and youth custody centre residents were burglary, theft and car theft and it was not uncommon for young people to be charged with all three types of offence at one hearing. Only a small proportion had been charged or found guilty of crimes of violence, although more violent offenders were found in the remand centre than in the youth custody centre. Additionally, a few young people charged or convicted of the serious crime of murder were remanded in custody at the time of study.

The prison department records also provided a guide to the location of the inmate's home community. The following table illustrates the geography of the 27 courts used to process the inmates of both institutions. They are widely dispersed and indicate that, in some instances, one inmate's home will be more than 70 miles from another's. The study population included those from the inner city and from very rural settings. Moreover, even those who live within a few miles of each other came from areas with a distinct culture. So, whilst residents may share social class, their parent culture will be rather more diverse.

A significant proportion, 38 per cent, of the study population had been processed by one court in a large city (number one in table 5.10) and two thirds lived within an area 12 to 22 miles, as the crow flies, from the two institutions (indicated by the box in table 5.10). However, it is emphasised that the crow would probably get to the remand and youth custody centre far quicker than the prisoner's family and friends, especially when they are reliant on public transport. Although relatively near to home, most prisoners were emotionally distant from their family and friends.

Table 5.10 Geographical location of courts processing inmates

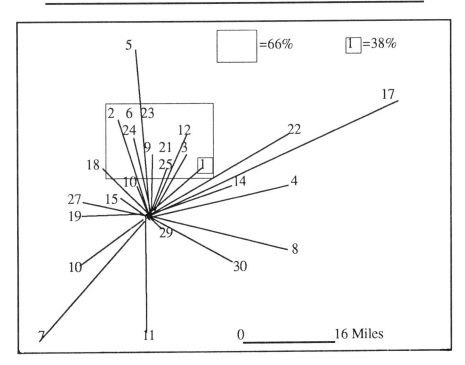

Conclusions

In this chapter, the characteristics of those young people whose criminal career has led them to prison custody have been charted using information from other studies and government statistics but also from prison files and records in the two institutions participating in the research for this book. As the following pages relate, the findings support much of what the inmates say in interviews. To begin with it is found that only a tiny minority of burglaries lead to young males being remanded or sentenced to custody. Indeed, as the Cambridge Study in Delinquent Development found, it is extremely rare for young people to persist with crime into adulthood. However, once young 14-17 year old burglars make their way into the prison system, they will find themselves with older, possibly more experienced, inmates including one or two who have been detained for serious offences, such as murder and rape. They are assembled in prisons which cater for boys from a wide geographical area and who, despite their common social class, share divergent cultural experience.

Inmates bring to the institutions a range of experiences. Some have been sentenced by a court as many as 15 times in the past, others are facing their first conviction. Many (54%) have been to detention centre or subject to a supervision (43%) or care order (28%), others have scant knowledge of treatment regimes. Indeed, the evidence on prisoners' characteristics would suggest that it is most difficult to assemble a specific history which is common to a group of entrants to remand and youth custody centres.

It is clear that youth custody residents will be well acquainted with prison life for, whilst experienced offenders can be ignorant of residential care, those under scrutiny in this book had been placed in at least one, sometimes a number of local prisons and remand centres before allocation to an open or closed institution.

Other features about the formal response to young offenders are of note. There is no strict tariff of disposals adhered to by the courts and similar offences may result in differing sentences as the court exhausts its options in its attempts to divert the young offender away from his chosen avenue. Success with this group is poor and an exponential pattern of court appearances and almost constant surveillance from the agencies of welfare and control is found.

Finally, although this study is concerned with property offenders, it is difficult to see them as a distinct category. A majority of inmates had, at some stage in their career, been charged with burglary (85%) and/or car-theft (52%). It is noteworthy that whilst these types of offenders try their hand at a range of misdemeanours, involvement in other more serious crimes such as violence (16%) or rape (2%) are not very common amongst this group.

It is clear that the subjects of this study enjoy unusual life experiences. The younger inmates of the remand and the youth custody centre under scrutiny had indulged in a range of crimes, coming into contact with various agencies of welfare and control and eventually finding themselves living with older, more experienced offenders who come from a wide geographical area. Thus, although the analysis of the episodes of the criminal career and the rules of criminal and delinquent behaviour will reveal an identity which has common features for the entire population under scrutiny, specific components may differ markedly. As is so often the case when looking back over successful professional careers, there are several unusual stops and starts which can be conveniently lost in a well constructed *curriculum vitae.*

The young people under scrutiny persistently break the law but there is scant evidence to suggest that their criminality becomes more serious or that they are moving up a tariff of offences. Few have been convicted of crimes of violence and although they move across a range of misdemeanours, they do not become involved in grave crimes such as murder or rape. Nonetheless, they have to cope with and adapt to a range of harsh and uncomfortable settings which takes them away from home and restricts their liberty. The following chapters which explore, in some depth, the young person's interpretations of his predicament may help to explain how the inmate continues his career in the face of a variety of responses which aim to turn him off his chosen path.

Summary Points

1. As a society we do not lightly send our young to prison. It is estimated that for every 1,000 burglaries only 24 young males will be sent to a remand centre and/or youth custody in 1988.
2. The Cambridge Study shows that a high proportion of adolescents are delinquent but few persist with the behaviour and that whilst most adult prisoners were adolescent recidivists, not all adolescent recidivists become adult prisoners.
3. The remand and youth custody centres cater for offenders of varying age and experience including a tiny minority on remand for grave crimes.
4. The study population do not share a common experience of the justice system. A few are relatively inexperienced, others are old campaigners.
5. The prisoners have experienced a range of disposals from the courts, some categories have fewer numbers than might be expected eg., only one-third have been subject to a care order as a result of offences. Other categories are oversubscribed; for instance, nearly two-thirds have been to a detention centre.

6. One disposal can involve a number of career moves and the youth custody inmates experience 2.5 prison placements as part of their last court sentence.

7. The career maps show that some prisoners are new to residential care and that there is no clear tariff of disposals. A fine or a caution can follow a youth custody sentence. For those with long experience of the courts, the pattern of appearances is exponential and periods of liberty or freedom from statutory observation reduce over time.

8. Certain types of disposal are linked with others in the criminal career, eg., detention centre and attendance centre orders, community service orders and youth custody.

9. Involvement in different types of crime changes with age, eg., crimes of violence against the person is most commonly committed by those aged 17-20. Burglary is most frequently committed by young people aged 14-16 years.

10. Usually, inmates commit a number of crimes crossing a number of categories, eg., many burglars are also car thieves. However, convictions for violence are relatively uncommon.

11. The sample population is geographically dispersed and one cell in the remand centre may contain inmates whose homes are 70 miles apart. Even those who live close to each other may come from distinct cultures. Many inmates are physically near to home but emotionally distant.

6. Early days in the criminal career

In this chapter, the first steps in a criminal career which lead persistent property offenders to custody are charted. Evidence on the response of family and friends to delinquency which runs counter to sub-cultural theory is described. Over time, a young person persisting with delinquency becomes estranged from and develops new roles within the local community. This chapter lays out the rules of behaviour which characterise this transition and re-examines the theoretical propositions explored in this study in the light of new evidence presented.

In the following pages the lives of persistent young property offenders prior to their admission to custody are considered. This chapter focuses upon the period during which they come under the scrutiny of statutory authorities, followed in Chapter Seven by the period of time when further offending is highly likely to result in a remand or sentence to custody. Interviews with 45 young people incarcerated in a remand and a youth custody centre are used to illustrate points extrapolated using the framework earlier described. Other writers' work on the individual's ability to choose and persist with a career will also act as a valuable aid.

Indeed, it will be seen that there is considerable research evidence which suggests that it is common for adolescents to contravene the laws of the state. Choosing to offend is not unusual among young people. However, deciding to participate in more serious crime such as a burglary is a different matter. This is a very unusual activity for adolescents and it is rarer still to find young people who persist with this behaviour. This chapter will clarify how the subjects under scrutiny arrive at offending decisions.

The principal focus will, however, be to reveal and understand influences upon the criminal identity. How, for example, do persistent offenders respond and adapt to the poor view held of them by family and friends? How does their identity correlate with their behaviour patterns? Research has shown that delinquents' descriptions of their situation do not always correspond to reality and, in the coming chapters, considerable attention will be devoted to the way in which young offenders re-interpret events. Finally, whilst it is hoped to chart changes in the identity of the young offender in each of the four episodes under scrutiny, a proposition that is supported by other research evidence, it may also be possible to note developments within each episode.

In this chapter, these questions, together with the process of becoming an 'outsider' and the way in which young offenders come to perceive themselves as separate from others are dealt with. Beginning with an examination of early criminal behaviour, it will be shown that experiments with law-breaking provide few material benefits but great emotional satisfactions for the participants. However, the subjects of this study persist with delinquency despite hesitant peers and family wrath and possible reasons for such continuity in behaviour will be revealed. Overall, this chapter will bear witness to the gradual social isolation of young property offenders destined for penal custody.

First steps onto the career ladder

There have been numerous studies, both in the United Kingdom and in the United States, which show that the vast majority of young people transgress societal laws (eg. Osbourne and West 1978). However, this evidence is reliant upon tests of self-reported delinquency which cover a range of indictable and non-indictable offences, most of which are very minor, for example riding a bicycle at night without lights. As previously stated evidence illustrates, although most young people are vulnerable to entry into a criminal career, few succumb. It has also been seen that a sizeable part of the juvenile justice system is now devoted to diverting minor offenders away from statutory supervision, so that those who do come to the notice of the courts are likely to be persistent delinquents charged with relatively serious offences, for example stealing cars or burglary. There is a considerable gap between everyday delinquency and the crime that precipitates the subjects of this study towards prison.

When prisoners in the remand and youth custody centre were asked to describe the first time they broke the law, all -without exception- set forth an event of relative seriousness and nobody mentioned the bicycle offences and chocolate bar stealing that almost certainly preceded the offence mentioned. Moreover, all of the respondents described an event which they got away with and evaded police detection.

A number of other characteristics are common to the description of the 'first crime', some of which become apparent in the following quotations from a car thief and a burglar.

'Yeh I was hanging around with this kid. And he came down the road in this car, and I said 'Whose is that?' And he said 'It's easy'. And then I said 'Can I have a go?', and he said 'Yeh'. So I took my time and he told me what to do, 'cos at first you don't know what to do. So I put it in first and I was going down the road, going about 20 miles an hour. And he said 'Put it into second' and so I put it into second and I was going about 40 miles an hour then. Then we came to an island and I didn't know what to do and I pushed my foot down on the accelerator and we hit this island and the car turned over. And we got out and got right out of it.... I remember it was such a laugh.... No, I cannot remember what made me do it.'

'Yeh, we moved down to (suburb of large city). And it's the old story; I got mixed in with some kids. Right? When I first knew them I just used to hang about, doss about. And then somebody said 'Oh we've got no money', and we got to doing a job. Well, we weren't bothered what we were going to get, so I went to a shop, (name of shop) up (District of large City) and I went round the back with me mates. We got to break in round the back door. And we got in and we got suits and coats and things like that. And it was good, but we didn't get no money and we had to dump all the suits and the coats, they were no good to us. But we never got caught. Did you ask me what I'd been caught for?'

These responses to the question about the inmate's first transgression of the law are similar to most others recorded during the fieldwork and demonstrate important features of young offenders' behaviour. Initially, it is clear that the particular event chosen by the inmate is memorable to him. The offence described is never committed alone and often involves groups of four or five, occasionally more, and follows a period of 'hanging around, doing nothing', a reminder of the work of Shibutani (1966) and Cohen (1972) on groups of youngsters waiting to be entertained. The evidence also suggests that, early in the career, offenders have little idea about criminal techniques, for example, what to steal, how to drive a stolen car or how to dispose of stolen property profitably and, consequently, derive little material benefit from their exploits. Let us look at these points in more detail.

Early criminal activity is at the forefront of the young prisoner's mind. The inmates excitedly describe their early exploits, emphasising the funny and ridiculous aspects. The event seems to hold some significance, but it is not taken very seriously.

The excitement has been generated by a group of people, for none of the descriptions of the 'first crime' involved a lone offender. Moreover, the respondent usually describes himself as a passive member of the group, taken along for the ride, status and machismo under test. The sense in which others 'dare' the young recruits to participate is very apparent in the interviews, as one young person explains, 'If you could do something (criminal) you could show you meant business, even if you lifted (stole) something useless or got caught.' However, as later chapters reveal, experienced offenders are not in the habit of taking young apprentices along to help with and learn from criminal activity. This would seem to suggest that early offending involves groups of inexperienced youngsters. What role does the sub-culture play in the development of the criminal identity?

Reference groups (gangs)

At the outset, it should be noted that the fieldwork for this study gathered little information which would support the suggestion that 'gangs' of young people frequent our streets, at least not in the same form as exists in the United States (Campbell 1984, Marsh and Campbell 1982, Whyte 1943). Instead, from the perspective of the persistent young offender, small groups of local boys will occasionally come together to produce a gang. For example;

> 'If you were going out on a Saturday night, and there was enough of you, and you were going down the City Centre, then there would be about 10 of you. At least 10, because it's down the City Centre. But if you're just hanging around the area then there will be two or three of you.'

As well as numerical differences, the activities and features of gangs and groups are also distinct. The former might have a name, masculine and geographically distinct; for example, 'W_____ Lumber Lads,' which can be spray-painted on a suitably anomic wall. Larger groups meet very infrequently but their existence is important to local youngsters in the sense that they provide a vehicle through which notions of territory and competitiveness between communities are emphasised. Thus, they are often associated with aggression. For instance,

> 'You don't have to be in a big group and most of the time you're not. But if there's going to be a fight, you know, then obviously there'll be a big group of us, because, other people from other areas come down and, if you're on your own, you get the shit kicked out of you. So if it's a fight, it's two big groups.'

As the literature survey suggested, small groups are more common. Hanging around in parties of two or three, 'doing nothing' is consistently referred to by those interviewed for this research. Such groups have no names or special purpose, for example to protect territory and they are not intrinsic to crime, although they do have a role to play in criminal activity. These groups also have a number of other functions. Adolescent gatherings are important manifestations of the informal social system where each individual has a contribution to make and where rules agreed by the participants are as important as laws created by the state and enforced by adults. It will be seen that Sutherland and Cressey's (1970) code and value system described in Chapter Four will be instrumental in the maintenance of such groups.

Although the 'first crime' described by the participants in this research is relatively serious, the descriptions reveal similarities with findings on petty delinquency in that the activity appears to follow periods of hanging-around 'doing nothing'. As a young person remanded to custody explains,

> 'You'll be down the park and having a game of baseball, or a game of football or something,...... somebody will say 'Do you fancy going down for a bit of knock-off?' or we'll decide to get some colour tellies or something. It's like that for the first few times.'

There is little, if any, preparation for crime, nor many ideas about where the activity will lead. As the previous examples illustrate, there are many possible outcomes. The car thieves risk killing innocent victims and could easily find themselves on a manslaughter charge, depending upon whom or what the car hit.

Early on, offenders have little idea about what to do; the car thieves cannot drive, the burglars do not know what to steal or how to dispose of the booty. As a consequence, most of the stories have an unhappy ending, a crashed car, a speedy exit or, as one of the previous respondents recounts, a collection of jackets and suits which would appear conspicuous and inappropriate when worn by the inner-city skinhead. 'We nicked these suits, I don't know why, and when we got them home they were all about ten sizes too big, they were useless.'

Nonetheless, although few of those questioned were able to record any material benefit from their early expeditions into relatively serious crime, most appear to have enjoyed the experience. Crawling from an over-turned car or being chased by the victims of a burglary are not events which many would recall with any fondness, yet, for the young offender who pursues a career through prison department establishments, they evoke satisfaction. One example from an interview with an inmate illustrates these points.

> 'I was on glue and I robbed these cars, about nine of them, one after the other with my mate. At first I couldn't drive, I felt sick, I had diarrhoea and stomach pains, I was shitting myself. When I got to the cop station, I had to stand up at the bar and I couldn't stand up man, my legs were going like jelly; that was one of the best times.'

The response of family and friends

It may be that participation in relatively serious crime, such as car theft or burglary, is fairly common amongst certain groups of adolescents. If this is the case, few are prepared to repeat the experience, otherwise our jails would be even fuller than they already are. But the persistent nature of criminality is probably the most salient feature to set apart those living in remand and youth custody centres. In their descriptions of early criminal activity, young prisoners emphasise a fairly delinquent home community and many are able to recall fathers or other family members being sentenced to custody. Perhaps family and peers encourage continuity in offending patterns?

The evidence from interviews in the remand and youth custody centre lends little support for this sub-cultural perspective. Indeed, family and peers appear to distance themselves from those who continue to offend. For example, the intrusion of the agencies of welfare and control into the lives of the family causes upset and tension even when prison has been a familiar refuge. As one young prisoner explained,

> 'My dad (who had been to prison) says, 'there's nothing big in going to borstal you know? I've done it.... There's nothing big in being a fuckin' crook', like that.... I love my mum and dad, we're as close as ever, but even though he's been inside, he's really hard about me being inside, it's as if it's different for him. They don't want to help you when you've been in trouble, they don't want to know it's happened.'

Local friends, sometimes burglars or car-thieves, also become hesitant. Few young people progress from occasional to persistent offending and those who do make the transition become isolated within, but not excluded from, their peer group. As the following chapters show, adolescents find crime intriguing and, consequently, the activity carries certain prestige for the participants and delinquents persisting in the face of prosecution gather particular renown. However, for all their tolerance, adolescents' views on persistent delinquency are seldom complimentary and the inmates in the remand and the youth custody centre were aware of their 'bad press'.

> 'They talk about me, you know. They say, 'Oh look at him the stupid bastard, he's always getting into trouble'. They're good kids but they talk about me like that 'Oh, he's fuckin' nicked again. It's a shame for him'. You know, 'he don't need to do it, he can't help it.'

Re-defining a local role

As local boys change their views of the persistent offender, so the persistent offender changes his view of the petty offender. Those with a first foot firmly on the criminal ladder begin to attach status to offences committed by friends and acquaintances and to dismiss or play-down events at the lower end of this constructed tariff. For example, in the following description of a minor offence committed by an inmate's friend the offence is totally dismissed.

> 'No, you couldn't say some of (my mates) have been in trouble. Like, R_____, he was in this fruit shop with his mate, and his mate chucked this melon through the window and this other kid picked it up. He went walking down the road with this melon. And he got done for receiving (laughing) receiving a stolen melon. So you couldn't really say they've been in trouble.'

Crime committed by family members is similarly graded. Thus, persistent young offenders find themselves distanced from family and friends; the persistent delinquent portrays himself as aloof from a family which, in turn, looks upon him with reproach. This growing apart is a gradual process and is accompanied by a more general sense of disaffection with the wider society. For example, many of the inmates expressed the opinion that society was prejudiced against them, not because of ethnicity or class, but because of their life-style. They felt picked upon by the police and made an example of by the court. Those who adopted a readily recognisable lifestyle felt persecuted for it. For example, one young person in the remand centre is able to rationalise the carrying of a dangerous weapon on this basis.

> ''Cos in (large city) like, there's a lot of prejudice. Like I'm a skinhead right? Now I don't ask other people about what they think but other people take it that all skinheads are prejudiced, but they are prejudiced themselves. And some, you can see them talking about you as you're walking about. And some, I live in a rough area of (suburb of large city) and, often you can't walk home with people pulling blades (knives) out on you, so you need a blade. Sounds fuckin' stupid but you do need them.'

There is a steady estrangement from family and friends throughout the criminal career but it is most clearly felt when the offender is caught. At this time his relationship with family and others in the community is subject to dramatic change. Friends will be vaguely interested, even excited at the young offender's misfortune, but the inmate perceives little sympathy in such concern. The family are catapulted into overt disapproval. Sometimes this is manifested in a closing of ranks, but when the police, social workers and solicitors have left the scene the young offender can receive a damning reception. As a youth custody centre resident explained,

> 'When they're all gone, nobody wants to know. You're just a stupid little bleeder who's got all the neighbours interested in your house. Nobody likes that do they? Like, if you were in a car crash everybody would feel sorry for you. But if you're in a car crash and you nicked the car everybody's not so sorry for you.'

Of course, one of the major consequences of being caught is the number of outside agencies who can be mobilised to intervene in the inmate's life. Police become very interested in his activities, reports will be written. He will have to go to court and solicitors will be involved. Depending upon the disposal of the court, he may be required to meet with social workers, probation officers, prison officers, intermediate treatment officers, victims of crime or other criminals. Being caught can result in acquaintance with many professionals with roles in the criminal justice system and it can remove the offender from other stabilising influences such as work or school colleagues. It certainly gives the drifting adolescent something to do.

External agencies were omnipresent in the accounts offered by prisoners; particularly for those who had sustained long relationships with probation officers or had been in local authority care or under supervision. As an example, a recent 16 year old arrival to the remand centre complained,

> 'What you lot don't know is that it's much more than just getting a hard time, you've got to feel guilty, you've got to think about the people you've nicked things from and you've got to go on doing this forever. No, my care order ends when I'm 18, but I could have left when I was 16. That would have been sound. I'd wanted to be rid of them since I was 11, man. Four years ago I was going good, 2-3 years to go, great man. And then in a few weeks I would have been through. But now this. Then after this it will be somewhere else and after that probation. Everybody's interested, you can't get away from them.'

This language of scrutiny and control would be largely unintelligible to the majority of sixteen year olds. The words describe victims, guilt, care orders, time to go before the 'sentence' ends, before release from enforced welfare and other interested agencies. Unfortunately for the offender, all interventions assume the mantle of control and interference. It is a language shared by a few who inhabit a separate world and each detention by the police and each appearance of the social worker re-emphasises this separateness.

Over time, the persistent delinquent seems to tire of the peer group who participated in his first delinquent excursions. Whilst early criminal activity amongst the inexperienced tends to involve groups, persistent offenders, by now well-known to the juvenile justice system, begin to engage in more solitary activity, occasionally involving one or two others. This has the triple benefits of reducing the chances of being caught, increasing the yield on the crime and maintaining by distance and mystery a certain notoriety.

'If there's three or four of you and you don't know what you're doing then you're going to fuck it up. Or if you don't fuck it up then somebody's going to scream about it and you're going to get caught. And then if you get 50 quid and there's one of you, you get 50 quid, or if there's two of you, you get 25, or if there's six of you, you get fuck all..... But they all know; they say 'where was he last night?' and all they've got to do is look in the paper and see what was done and they say 'Oh he's done that man', so everybody knows.... You don't even have to tell, they just know, but you carry on.'

Thus, it can be seen that persistent criminal activity leading to a court appearance is an unusual lifestyle and a cursory glance at the behaviour of the young offender is perplexing. He frequents a world filled with unpleasantness from which he might surely escape if only he would take the simple step of desisting from anti-social activity. Why does he persist? What rules underpin the behaviour of an offender who has decided to pursue a criminal career and do these help with an understanding of his criminal identity?

Rules of behaviour

At the beginning of this study, a method was outlined which exposes the criminal identity by breaking down the criminal career into composite episodes and by focusing upon the rules which guide the behaviour in each of these episodes. This chapter has discussed the offender's progress during the first of four episodes during the criminal career, during which he has first participated in relatively serious crime. In subsequent chapters, three further episodes will be scrutinized, including life on the margins of prison.

As previously outlined, four types of rule can be identified to be operating in each episode. These are; societal rules, which change little in different situations and apply equally in the community and in custody; formal rules which are publicly stated but which reflect the context in which they are applied; belief rules which act as informal guides to the offender's thinking about his situation; and, interaction rules which guide the offender in his various liaisons. The ten most prominent rules in each category are listed in this chapter. These lists of rules reflect the interview transcripts, indeed, in a number of instances the rule is a re-statement of something inmates have said. As such, the lists may appear simplistic but they have been arrived at using a long-considered theoretical framework and are considered to be accurate reflections of the types of guidelines used by young persistent property offenders.

It should be clear that these rules act only as a guide. The persistent delinquent need not follow them should he not choose to. Indeed, breaking societal and formal rules are part of his life-style. It also becomes apparent that different types of rule can be incongruous with each other, indeed any inconsistencies between rules will form an integral part of the understanding of the criminal identity of the young offender presented in this study.

Let us now turn to a discussion of the rules in each of the four areas.

Societal rules

Initially, it is clear that the great majority of the young offender's life is crime-free. As the previous chapter has shown, the inmates surveyed for this study appear in court, on average, four times over a three and half year period. This data also reveals that at each court appearance, a mean of 4.4 crimes are dealt with, including those 'taken-into-consideration'. Young offenders are not arrested for every crime they commit and most questioned for this research claimed two criminal excursions for every detection. It is certainly unlikely that they evade police attention three times for every arrest, but this figure can act as a safe guide.

From these statistics it is possible to calculate that the young offender who spends a sojourn in prison department custody will commit 52 crimes over a period of four years (4 x 4.4 x 3); thirteen a year, just over one a month. Moreover, crime occurs in sprees, it is not a regulated activity. Thus, it is safe to say that each persistent young offender has plenty of crime-free time, possibly going many months without breaking the law and, in the early stages at least, there will be many pressures upon the young offender to conform and observe the law.

Nonetheless, the young offenders will break or risk breaking many of the societal rules listed below. They not only indulge in car theft and burglary but they also risk facing a manslaughter charge if the car hits a pedestrian or aggravated burglary if the occupant of the house unexpectedly returns. It does not seem as though the grave consequences of the offending are very well thought out by the delinquents.

Societal rules

1. Do not offend
2. Do not steal
3. Do not injure
4. Do not break into houses
5. Do not steal from cars
6. Do not take and drive away cars
7. Do not kill somebody when you steal a car
8. Do not break into a house when somebody is in the house
9. Feel guilty for the things you have done wrong
10. Feel that offending is unjust

Formal rules

If, in the heady moments of the crime, the young offender is unaware that he has transgressed any societal laws, there are many people only too anxious to remind him of his duty. This may occur before the offender has been caught, for example a family may be reluctant to turn to the police but eager to remind their son of the plight of the victim. When the statutory authorities become involved, the offender will be faced with a new set of formal rules to do with the police, courts, statutory supervision and, possibly, residential care. Again and again it will be emphasised that offending is bad, unjust, wrong and hurtful to the victim. As one inmate explains, 'You've only nicked a car but when you're in that court every fucker has his say, so you'd think you'd shot the fuckin' Pope.'

Being caught crystalises events for the delinquent and, during this episode, the formal rules are essentially a re-statement of the societal rules, a reminder to the offender that he has over-stepped the mark and would do well to reform quickly. However, even at this stage some incongruity between the societal and formal rules are necessary as we attempt to give the petty offender a second chance and accept first misdemeanours as a temporary misconduct never to be repeated. As a society we bend the rules, we say 'it is OK just this once, but don't do it again'.

Formal rules

1. Be concerned for the victim of your crime
2. If you offend, do not offend again
3. If you offend, go to court
4. If you offend, change schools

5. If you offend, meet the victim
6. If you offend, be supervised by a social worker or probation officer
7. If you offend, benefit from the advice of a solicitor
8. If you offend, you will be punished
9. Give the petty offender a second chance
10. If you offend more than three times you can expect to go to prison

Belief rules

As the following list illustrates, the belief rules used by young offenders during this episode in their criminal career are very different from the publicly stated rules. At this stage, offending is unplanned and reaps little material gain but it is a new, exciting and usually enjoyable experience which should not be taken too seriously. The inmates in the remand and youth custody centres chatter easily about early delinquency but they seldom give any thought to the victims of their crime, the people who lose their videos, hi-fi's and cars. Indeed, many of the inmates interviewed during the course of the research felt unclear about what they should feel guilty for or about whom they should feel remorse. One inmate explained that, 'You can't remember why you broke into the house, what you took or whose house it was so why should you care?' Throughout the transcripts there is a signal absence of sympathy for the victims of crime. Crime is re-defined so that excitement is maximised and the role of the victim minimised. The criminal is left with nothing to feel guilty about and with nobody violated.

However, towards the end of this episode surrounding the offender's first participation in relatively serious crime the belief rules are beginning to change. The young offenders discussed in this study have continued with these behaviour patterns despite the growing disapproval of friends and outright condemnation of family. As he gets further along the career route, the persistent delinquent must learn rules of behaviour which allow continuity of delinquency in the face of discouragement and to conduct himself in the community as an 'outsider'. He will appear unconcerned about the unease of family and friends and complain about the prejudice others hold about his behaviour. He will appear unruffled by the growing number of professionals who frequent his life and begin to use the language of a criminal, emphasising the time he has to serve on his sentence and the minor complexities of the law which has circumscribed his freedom. As a number of prisoners stated during interviews, 'the main thing is not to take it all too seriously.' Thus, it is already clear that the belief rules which act as an informal guide to the offender's behaviour in this episode are likely to be very different from those which operate in the following episode.

Belief rules

1. Occasionally engage in crime for a bit of fun
2. Do not worry about what you are going to steal
3. Do not worry about why you are stealing something
4. Do not worry about what you are going to do with the goods you steal
5. The goods you steal need not be valuable
6. Do not worry about the consequences of your crime
7. Get as much excitement as you can out of the event
8. Commit offences in groups
9. Choose groups with a similar experience of crime
10. Do not take the event too seriously

Interaction rules

In the early stages of the criminal career and particularly the episode studied in this chapter, delinquency is characterised by groups of adolescents experimenting with formally stated laws. In describing their exploits, the young people play down the importance of the event when talking to family but maximise the excitement of the offence when discussing it with peers. Generally, in the early part of this episode, the rules which guide what the young person says about his delinquency are very similar to those which guide his criminal beliefs. In describing crimes to peers, the young offenders appear unconcerned about failure, amongst friends they are lured into delinquency for the sake of not losing face.

However, this chapter has also witnessed the growing unease among friends of those who persist with the life-style. Prisoners claimed that concern grows over time,

'at first you can get away with it, you can say you won't do it again, you didn't know what you were doing and all that crap and sometimes they (the family) will see the funny side of it; and your mates always think it's a laugh. But later, you're more on your own like.'

Indeed, the persistent offender becomes aloof, those who desist from the delinquent way of life are treated with disdain and their delinquency considered to be trivial and minor. As the delinquency is experienced and described as trivial excitement, the belief and interaction rules are in harmony for most of this episode. However, as the offender continues with the behaviour it will be seen that these two types of rule become increasingly out of tune.

Interaction rules

1. Be willing to fail
2. Do not worry about being caught
3. Be unconcerned about family discouragement, chastisement
4. Be unconcerned about the prospect of being punished
5. Say you will not offend again
6. Say you did not realise what you were doing
7. Say you did it for a bit of fun
8. Emphasise the funny, less serious aspects of the event
9. Say that you didn't think about the victims
10. Say that you didn't think of the consequences of your actions

Conclusions

The first steps into a criminal career have been explored in this chapter. How do the rules of behaviour just identified help us to understand concepts the delinquent has about himself, that is to say his criminal identity and how do these data impinge upon the theoretical propositions earlier outlined?

The focus has not been upon petty offences, such as minor shop-lifting, but upon burglary and car-theft. Initially, it can be seen that these first serious excursions across the rule of law are memorable to prisoners who fondly reminisce about inexperienced groups stumbling into strangers' property as an alternative to doing nothing.

However, whilst groups are instrumental to early crime, their response to those who persist with offending can only be described as lukewarm-warm. This evidence would suggest flaws in some sub-cultural explanations of delinquency. Indeed, the family can become outraged when police and social workers become involved and the pressures from the home area are to conform rather than to break social expectations.

Over time, the persistent property offender begins to disengage from the local scene and attach status to others' offences. The estrangement is rammed home each time he is caught, taken to the police station, has to appear in court and to participate in a range of reformatory schemes. He meets new acquaintances, begins to develop a specialized language and forms a different relationship with the wider society. Let us briefly re-consider the theoretical propositions outlined in the opening chapter in the light of this evidence.

There is considerable data in this chapter which support the proposition that persistent young property offenders choose a criminal career based upon a series of decisions which appear to the young person to be rational. At this stage the rationale is excitement and enjoyment rather than the acquisition of material goods. The decision making in the early stages is collective; however, the evidence does not suggest that young offenders inherit their delinquency from the local culture. Early criminal activity does take place within the local community and their offending will be tolerated by peers, if not by their family. The patterns of early delinquency fit into normal adolescent development discussed in Chapter Four: the offences are committed by small groups of two or three, occasionally four, five or six. It is recognized as a 'bit of fun' and there is little material benefit to be gained.

A different set of decisions will be used by the offender who decides to continue with delinquency beyond the first arrest. As the previous chapter has shown, there are in operation well thought-out measures to divert youngsters away from the juvenile justice system. However, once caught, the young offender can exchange teacher for a police officer, the classroom for a court and, in certain circumstances, school for custody. He will experience a series of reprisals which will attempt to fan feelings of guilt, shame and remorse. Furthermore, as the coming chapters will reveal, in attendance centres, local authority residential centres, whilst doing community service or in prison, the persistent criminal is very likely to meet others who persist with crime. Although the offender may be distanced from his local community, he will find solace with others who cope with similar problems. Thus, the justice system may, in a number of ways, contribute to the criminal identity.

The coming chapters will also demonstrate that friends introduced by the justice system do not always display the excitement expressed by friends in the local community when crime is described. A competitive element is injected into the interaction and the recent entrant to the criminal career will have to present his own exploits in new and interesting ways. It is at this stage that the persistent delinquent begins to learn and adopt strategies which confuse observers of his behaviour. As the coming chapters demonstrate, descriptions offered to the *cognoscenti* differ markedly from those given to the innocent.

There is, then, evidence to support the proposition that shared guidelines are important in the choice of the criminal identity. How congruous is this identity with the behaviour? The identification of the rules of behaviour in each episode will help with an answer to this question. During this episode of the criminal career, the societal rules are re-reinforced by and are in relative harmony with the formal rules publicly stated by the family and the statutory authorities. For the most part, those belief rules which guide the behaviour of a criminal are very similar to the interaction rules. The delinquency is both viewed and described as petty, unplanned, exciting and enjoyable occasional excursions, possibly never to be repeated.

However, it is possible to forecast changes in the rules used by the young people within this early episode of the criminal career. Moreover, these changes are likely to lead to growing incongruity between what the offender does and his descriptions of his activity.

Summary Points

1. When prisoners were asked to describe the first time they broke the law, all without exception, described an event of relative seriousness.
2. This initial delinquency is committed in small groups, follows periods of hanging around 'doing nothing' and is characterised by lack of planning and knowledge.
3. Early criminal expeditions are remembered with some affection by inmates who recall the excitement the event generated at the time.
4. Small groups of young people who occasionally come together to form larger groups is the common pattern of association amongst adolescents at this stage in the career. Such groups have a number of functions and are not intrinsic to crime.
5. The evidence from this study does not suggest that family and peers encourage continuity in offending patterns. Indeed, the converse is true. There is a steady estrangement from family and friends throughout the criminal career, a pattern clearly emphasised when the young offender is caught.
6. One of the major consequences of being caught is the intervention of statutory authorities. External agencies were omnipresent in the accounts offered by prisoners who adopt an argot and style which reflect their deep knowledge of the juvenile justice system; an argot and style which would be unintelligible to most adolescents.
7. Over time, the persistent delinquent becomes increasingly solitary in his offending behaviour, a feature which reflects a reluctance of peers for continuing participation in crime, and a desire to maximise the returns from the criminal activity.
8. The ten most prominent societal, formal, belief and interaction rules operating in this episode have been listed and discussed.
a) Societal rules are still strong; although his lack of skill incurs the risk of serious offence or injury, the majority of the offender's life is still crime free.
b) Being caught introduces the offender to a range of formal rules to do with the police, court and the plight of the victim.

c) The belief rules reveal the lack of planning in early crime and its generation of excitement for the participants. However, changes in these rules which allow persistence in the behaviour pattern are already apparent.

d) Interaction rules also change during this episode as offenders switch from maximising the excitement from the crime in conversation with peers to playing down the event as they cope with the growing unease of family and friends.

7. On the margins of prison

This chapter is concerned with a further episode in the criminal career. Offending patterns, social identity and networks of the persistent delinquent are highlighted. During this chapter the increasing involvement of statutory authorities and the ability of young prisoners to re-interpret life experiences to make the best of a poor situation are noted. The rules that guide the behaviour of an offender who fails to take routes which divert him away from custody are listed and commented upon. The theoretical propositions laid out in the opening chapter are re-examined in the light of new evidence.

Once he has embarked on his criminal career, how does the criminal identity of the young offender develop? In this chapter the young offender's offending patterns, presentation of self and social networks are considered. The way in which persistent delinquents contemplate prison is explored, together with their techniques for dealing with the statutory authorities. Finally, the rules of behaviour available as a guide to the young offender in this episode are listed and discussed. It is found that on the margins of prison, there is greater correspondence between formal, publicly stated rules and those interaction rules used by the offender. However, there is also greater incongruity between belief and interaction rules.

The chapter begins with an examination of aspects of the young person's criminality, for example whether he plans his delinquent excursions. More general aspects of personality are also highlighted and, for instance, it is discovered that competitiveness and individuality are common traits. What are the social networks of the young offender? It will become clear that, whilst early experiments with crime often involve groups of adolescents, the offender who persists, despite the interest of welfare and control agencies, is a more solitary animal, sometimes 'working' with one other. In many cases, it appears that young offenders seek out others with a similar life-style, not to offend with, but to refer to. At each stage in the career, the social networks of the offender serve important functions, for example, they act as a reference group and they lead to the social networks through which stolen goods can be sold for cash.

During the episode under study in this chapter, on the margins of prison department custody, the young offender is relatively set in his ways. His close friends are those who share his experience as an outsider and there are well established relationships with other parts of the juvenile justice system upon which to draw. These features of the criminal identity of the young people will now be explored in more detail.

Offending patterns

On a superficial level, at least, during this episode offenders see themselves as helpless beings, pushed along a conveyor belt towards ever more difficult times. They consistently present their criminality as increasing in seriousness. For example,

> 'I don't know, you just go up in the scale man, you just go up as you get older. Like it starts off with TDA's (car thefts), then assaults, then stabbing, and the lot. It just goes up and you just end up like that. I don't know. There's no reason why I should be that way, but there it is.'

In reality, unless one perceives car theft to be more innocuous than burglary or shop-lifting to be more injurious than criminal damage, young offenders' crime does not get 'worse'. These types of non-violent crimes tend to predominate and although the young who frequent remand and youth custody centres try their hand at a range of such activities and are arrested for a variety of offences, there are few who graduate from car theft to grievous bodily harm.

Nor is there any evidence to suggest that criminality gets worse in terms of the value of the goods involved, an important denominator in sentencing those found guilty of crimes of theft. Targets chosen by young thieves and court disposals vary and a house burglary raising £500 which results in a fine in his fifteenth year may well be followed by the theft of an empty handbag from a car and dispatch to detention centre in his sixteenth year. The criminal career is not a smooth journey, it is a series of bumps and starts.

Accounts in the last chapter revealed inexperience, events tended to be unexpected and carried the hall-mark of a 'moral holiday'. However, when inmates are asked to describe their last criminal excursion, greater confidence is shown and the event is viewed as the product of skill and experience meeting with opportunity. For instance,

> 'I went down this mate's house and he had a Peugeot motor car. Well it weren't running or anything and they wanted me to fix it. 'Cos that's what I'm good at, fixing cars. So I got it running and there was this bloke down there. I'd never met him before in my life and I got talking to him and I went down to see him again the next day. Well, we got talking about doing some job, you know, just running in, snatching the money and running out. But anyway, he

says 'do you wanna come?'. And I was trying to get a flat with my girlfriend and I thought 'get the money, it'll pay for this flat' So I says 'Yeh'. I went down to the shop in (suburb of large city) and we were wearing these stocking masks and he brought this bread knife with him..... We says 'give us the money', she says 'the till don't open', so I picked the till up and ran out, we chucked it in the car and left.'

The above quotation embodies the assertiveness offenders display when describing criminal activity in this episode. There are fewer expressions of excitement about an act which is quite out of the ordinary even among regular offenders. The opportunity for the crime came by chance, although it would not present itself to those without criminal experience. Here, the offender takes a 'moral holiday' but the excursion is to a place he has visited four or five times in the past and he is well acquainted with the language and local customs.

This recent criminal activity is highly likely to precipitate the offenders towards custody and they are beginning to assert clearer limits to their behaviour and their crime is characterised by a modicum of planning. For example, some more experienced burglars will not break into houses in their own locality and many expressed an aversion to Council owned residences, although such preferences are usually based upon mercenary rather than ideological beliefs. For example,

'I don't know, it's because we all live in Council houses, so we just don't do it to them. I mean, where we're living it's quite normal, so we don't have the kind of stuff that's worth knocking off. Like they (Council houses) 'ain't got videos like most houses we've done, we just can't afford that sort of thing.'

Moreover, by the time they arrive at the remand and youth custody centre, young offenders are clearer about the details of their criminal activity. For example, they may prefer a particular type of car to steal or a certain time in the day for breaking into houses. There are attempts to plan crimes according to the tariff of disposals available to the court. For instance, many burglars steadfastly avoided occupied houses for fear of facing the serious charge of 'aggravated burglary'.

General preparation of this kind appears to be common, but for a crime to occur it is necessary for the plans to coincide with a suitable opportunity. In a subject area which does not lend itself easily to aetiology, the disposition to commit an offence at some point in the future is a most important 'cause' of crime. However, it should be emphasised that young offenders' planning is concerned with the general aspects of unlawful activity and seldom deals with the specific. Moreover, planning does not seem to lessen the propensity to get caught. Where inmates at the remand centre and the youth custody centre have been able to specify unlawful designs, these have often back-fired or collapsed in the heady moments of the event. Thus,

'You know Woolworths in (city suburb)? Well I planned that one. Not really a good plan, but I planned it. Looking back, it was a silly job really, because all I meant to do was get in and get some of those big radio sets, right? I'd been after one of them for ages and I knew where to off-load it. But they were all wired up, and there was display cabinets with all these 'Chunky dog' things in and I ended up getting those.'

The amount of adrenalin expended whilst breaking into the property of a stranger should not be under-estimated. Individually, inmates recall their crimes with some calm, but in groups the panic that besets the offender 'on the job' becomes clear. As one inmate explained,

'What you lot forget is that it takes a lot of bottle to swan into somebody else's house and lift all their gear, it scares the shit out of you and the first few times you do it you don't know what you're doing 'cos you're panicking right! But what you also forget is that once you've done it properly, it means something. Like you think it's wrong to do a burglary but even if you thought it was right you couldn't do it. So it's something.'

In many cases, it would seem that the panic leads to further unpleasantness for the victim of the burglary. A prison officer explained that,

'Yes, you get many insights, like I always wondered why they crap on the carpet when they are breaking and entering. It's because they are scared, they are worried sick. It makes you wonder why they do it.'

In a number of respects, the residents of the two prisons surveyed are very competitive and individualistic in their behaviour. Experienced offenders seldom seek co-operation of many others, they enjoy the status of 'outsider' in their own community and they tend to recoil from statutory interventions.

However, the interview transcripts reveal that early crime is little concerned with material gain and, although during this episode experience has bred success, the inmates do not seem destined for considerable wealth. It may be said that persistent young offenders see the challenge and excitement of the moment to be more important than the acquisition of capital and, in this sense, they bear a resemblance to young entrepreneurs. They live from day to day; they possess short-term goals and perspectives; they consistently hope that bad times will go away soon and that good times are just around the corner. However, their lives are also characterized by coherent patterns and, in many ways, they are aspirant.

So, the criminal identity develops during the fits and starts of the career. On the margins of prison, the offender's criminal excursions are still occasional, but the destination is now well known. He has the skill and experience to make the departure as soon as the right opportunity comes along. He begins to attempt a modicum of planning but designs often break down in the heady moments of the criminal act. Nonetheless, the persistent delinquent can appear aspirant and hopeful, the behaviour which reaps failure is beginning to be submerged in an identity which displays success. Let us look further at his criminal identity with an exploration of the social networks he enjoys.

Social networks

As he progresses along his chosen career, the persistent offender becomes increasingly solitary, at least as far as offending is concerned. However, the local sub-culture still retains two important functions during this episode of the criminal career. To begin with, peers provide a reference group to whom the offender can talk about his crimes, real and imaginary. This is clearly important to young offenders and, as the following quotation from a youth custody centre resident illustrates, there is some prestige to be gained.

'If you've been up to something then everybody gets to know about it, you never seem to be able to keep it quiet. So if you're hanging around that's what they wanna talk about. Some of your mates would never fuck about at all, some of them just haven't got the bottle, but they still want to know about it.'

Alternatively, as a remandee notes, the local reference group can provide relief when the 'pressures of the job' get too much.

'Sometimes you've done a house or something and it's on your mind and the police are on your back and you just want to get away from it. Then you go out with your mates, maybe go for a drink, anything really and you talk about it....'

Of course, these examples of the offender relating his criminal activity to members of the community are most ironic. Talking about crime clearly serves a number of important functions both for the offender and the listener. However, for the delinquent, it also increases his chance of being caught!

The introduction of planning into a crime can coincide with a reduction in the numbers participating in the event. A prisoner remanded to custody for a series of burglaries explains that

> 'I work with a mate, usually the same one. We take it in turns. We'll go up to a house and knock and say 'does so-and-so live here?' if there's somebody in, but if they're not then we are round the back and in through a window or something. We've got it fairly planned out, get the stuff straight out into a van or car and away. We can do up to four or five a day.'

Over time, the persistent burglar and car thief begins to break into social networks which can help to dispose of the products of criminal activity. As previous illustrations from interviews have shown, the material benefits from early crime are few, but time and experience lead to goods which must be marketed if they are to reap financial gain. The young offender quickly learns what to do with stolen video recorders, televisions, cars and motorbikes. For example,

> 'You get to find out who does the selling and then in time you get to do the selling. I do lots of selling you see, lots of kids they don't know how to, but I know. I used to go down the scrap yard and everybody in the scrap yard is thieves and I used to know they was thieves 'cos they'd have knocked off cars and they'd buy anything. And you don't go to one place; shop around and you get a good price.'

And, of course, these networks eventually suggest and, possibly, precipitate crime.

> 'Well if we robbed say an 'A' (1984) registered motor we could sell it. We could take the number plates off and respray it and we could sell it to a scrap merchant. But then you find out they want something else, like they wanted bikes and they ask you can you get 'this' and 'that', or you find out from your mates they want 'this' or 'that'.'

The cohesion and pre-planning between young offenders can be over-emphasised. In interviews in the remand and youth custody centre, prisoners demonstrated some assertiveness and acumen when talking about their own crimes and they felt secure about developing plans with one, possibly two, others. However, when larger groups of five prisoners are brought together to discuss and plan imaginary events, the result is chaos, indecision and argument. Thus, it would be foolish to suggest that the male young offender links into the existing, well-oiled machinery of crime. The relationship between the novices described in the study and professional crime mirrors that described by Humphries (1981) in his work on gangs at the turn of the century. As with so many of the contemporary offender's endeavours, the overwhelming impression is of one feeling his way through the dark.

Moreover, the nature of the activity militates against over-planning. As one inmate reminded another anxious to demonstrate how he thought and planned ahead, 'When you've got a stolen car you don't sit on it for a couple of weeks, you shift it quick.' Short-term goals are particularly important in the lives of these young people.

Whilst inmates at the two prison establishments under study claimed familiarity with other prisoners, they also perceived difficulties in maintaining friendships over time. Precise evidence in this area is very difficult to assemble, but it is highly probable that the persistent young offender known to the statutory authorities experiences many new friendship networks every year of his adolescent life. Although 'straight friends', that is those who do not offend or do not get caught, will shun their unlawful peers, another contributory factor is that the two groups are constantly separated by the criminal justice system eager to send the recalcitrant young on retreat to residential centres or remote communities.

Thus, when asked about their close friends, only a few names were given by each prisoner and common features applied to the characters described. Firstly, all those mentioned had committed an offence and most had appeared in court as a result of their misdemeanour. Secondly, although many had been to prison, all those described were at liberty when the study took place. A third feature of those described as close friends was their ability consistently to reappear throughout an otherwise transitory existence. In many cases this 'loyalty' was clearly consequent upon a parallel career through the juvenile justice system. Nevertheless, re-interpreted, poor outcomes can be viewed encouragingly.

> 'A close mate is somebody who will stick by you, right? Say you get in trouble and he was with you, the coppers don't know who it is and he'll say 'No, I weren't with him,' even though he was. And you'll say 'He never done nothing, it has nothing to do with him.' You both get sent down maybe, but that's good mates.'

On the other hand, as the following, seemingly bizarre, incident demonstrates, young offenders can be very positive in their will to maintain links with each other. Indeed, transport and distance are far less of a hindrance to friends than to relatives.

'It sounds silly like, but two lads who were here like, they both got nicked. They couldn't afford to come down and see me and this other lad. So they nicked a car to come down and see us. Then they ended up in here. It's stupid like, but that's the kind of friends you have. They did that just to come down and see us.'

The evidence collected to explore the theoretical propositions outlined in Chapter One suggests that as the young offender becomes more experienced, he develops into an increasingly solitary creature. However, in his formative years he has groups to which he can refer his behaviour and to whom he can turn for support. It would be wrong to assume that the persistent offender turns to others who offer wholesale condonation or to over-estimate the cohesion amongst such reference groups, but they are important components in the young offender's criminal identity. It is true, however, to say the offenders are never faced with the depth of relationship required to challenge and dispute another's chosen position, hence acceptance of any stupidity is assured.

During the latter stages of the episode considered in this chapter, the young person has established a link with wider criminal networks. By learning how to dispose of the proceeds of criminal endeavour, an important step in career development is made. In early criminal activity, the booty seldom fits the personal consumer needs of the young offender. When he is able to realise the financial gain for his endeavours the process assumes a different rationale. As one youth custody boy states, 'When you first start off you don't know why you do it, but when you've got £200 stuffed in your pocket it all seems to make sense.' However, the wad of cash is likely to lead to another problem; the impending detection and possible removal into prison detention.

Contemplating prison

This is a study of failures. The young people at the remand and youth custody centre who found their way into the sample population have been singularly unsuccessful at avoiding detection by the police. A little under half (48%) have appeared in court five times or more. Thus, they are not unused to police detention, court appearances or some form of state intervention including custody. For each crime the young person commits, there is the accompanying knowledge that detection is extremely likely.

However, the evidence does not suggest that the young offender is powerless in this process. Preceding extracts from interviews and their interpretation have shown that there is purpose in the young people's behaviour, although in many instances the outcome is unintended or less than satisfactory. The planning of the offender's delinquent activity can best be described as haphazard, but he is fully cognizant of the gravity of his behaviour and the negative view which numerous peers and adults have of his personality. The continuity in career found by Willis's (1977) school boys, who voluntarily entered a life of drudgery on the factory floor, is also apparent in the lives of young offenders who choose an identity of which prison is an integral part.

This is not to suggest that the prospective prisoner looks forward to incarceration. A prisoner explains that

> 'You can see that it's coming and you're warned about it. Like your mates say things like 'We done YC', 'I've done DC', 'I could do it standing on my hands' and every kid who comes out (of prison) says 'Oh it was easy' or 'No sweat.' But when they're inside, it's a different story, it's not time so much, it's just being away from your family. And you know that and that's what's waiting for you.'

Nonetheless, the young offender does not view his life experience as unbearable. He perceives certain events differently by re-interpreting previous experiences. This is particularly noticeable amongst those inmates who had been to community homes with education or other children's homes administered by local authority social service departments. Their reminiscences remind the listener of leavers from other, more affluent residential education settings, where control and formality are dressed up in embroidered anecdotes as anarchy and hedonism. For example, the following remandee describes to others a well known assessment centre.

> 'The assessment centre, you know the assessment centre, we cleaned the assessment centre clean of lead (laughing) carried it over the training school, up on to the training school roof. It was only a couple of wheelbarrows full..... The maintenance men went up to fix a leak, right, and (laughing) the roof was like that. It was good, man, they were good times. And me and B_____ were going to sell it. He's in here as well now. But they were good times.'

In Chapter Four, Matza and Sykes's (1957) theory that young offenders translate the meaning of their crimes and, for example, minimise the pain experienced by the victim was considered. The data collected for this study would also suggest that the experiences which follow being caught breaking the law are given new meaning by the young people, instance the way in which the pains of imprisonment are discounted. No doubt, whilst at liberty, prison is also perceived as an exciting episode. Indeed, all of these inmates interviewed who had previously been to detention centres gave the experience short shrift and accorded it low status. However, it is known from Home Office (1984c) research that the first few days at least are difficult to endure. Thus prisoners put a new interpretation upon past events and they become part of a coherent structure and pattern, part of life's rich pageant.

Dealing with statutory authorities

The young people considered in this study consistently break societal rules. Society's response is not, however, consistent. It is bound up in the bureaucracy of the juvenile justice system and the officers who administer that system. They apply what has been termed the formal rules of society, which are specific to particular social contexts, for example, the police station, the court, the social worker's office and so on. How does the offender, launched on a criminal career respond to these formal rules? As the following evidence illustrates, his relationship with the statutory authorities will differ depending upon the agency involved but, generally, there is a good deal of accord between the offender and the agents of welfare and control.

If, when committing crime young offenders act with purpose, they appear to be completely powerless when caught. No matter how experienced they are, few inmates expect justice and many claim that they have been unfairly treated either by the reduction of the severity of a charge to secure a plea of 'guilty' from the defendant or by the 'dumping' of others crimes when they are 'taken into consideration' on the charge sheet. The evidence for both these claims is scanty. However, it does indicate the way the inmates relate to their captors. For example,

'They know that I never touched any of those houses but I'm still being charged for it. But they've dropped the aggravated burglary. It's good of the coppers to drop it down to burglary. That's good of them to do that, but it's still wrong that I should take on all those TICs (crimes taken into consideration by the court).'

Within this arena, where the young offender wields little power, there may be a solicitor, perceptions of whom vary according to the individual involved. There will also be a social worker or probation officer, perceptions of whom are fairly uniform. For, amongst the prisoners interviewed for this research, blame for their present predicament was almost always accorded to the welfare officer. For example,

'(My Social Worker) came to see me three times to prepare me for court. The second time she said 'Hello' and then she said she'd better go now, like that. She said 'Hello, I hope you go well in court, I've got to go now.' Fucked off..... You know last time I saw her was when they were to pass sentence. She came just before the end of court. She came with her report, right. It was a shit report but she put it in all the same. Just before the end, right, you know what I mean?'

Within a coherent career, the police and the courts and, to a certain extent solicitors, have clearly defined roles for the young offender. He may be powerless to alter their judgements but he does understand their power. Social workers and probation officers are much more difficult to place and, divided by the walls and bars of a prison, the relationship can be particularly difficult.

To begin with, the welfare officer will carry the legacy of previous excursions across the legal divide or may even be associated with the crimes of other family members. Secondly, the social worker or probation officer is charged with gathering evidence to assemble a 'Social Enquiry Report' (SER) for the court, a process referred to by the young people as 'sniffing'. Thirdly, the welfare role gets lost among other procedures and, although the young people recognize difficulties, they cannot find anybody to turn to. As one youth custody centre resident notes,

'Obviously, you've got a problem, right? Now you can see where the problem was, but you can't solve it. You need someone to help you solve it.... someone you can rely on but there's just nobody who you can trust.'

Finally, all of these contradictions are manifest in the recommendation for sentence in the SER. The offender takes a dim view of any proposal for a custodial sentence. A sentence of custody will always reflect badly upon the author of the SER report, even when the bench ignore pleas for a community based alternative. But even if the social or probation officer succeeds in pleasing the client on one occasion, she or he is unlikely to maintain such a record over four or five court appearances. Thus, the welfare officer holds a cleft stick and is likely to reap the blame for the negative aspects of any court sentence, especially prison.

Rules of behaviour

The rules which guide behaviour during this episode of the career have again been identified from the transcripts of interviews with the young people. Once again, examples of ten rules operating in each of the four categories, societal, formal, belief and interaction, are given.

Societal and formal rules

The explicit rules operating during this episode differ little from those working in the previous episode. There are still hopes held that the young person will not re-offend and the expectations that the guilty will show remorse and penitence remain. The number of people representing the statutory authorities thrust into the young offender's life has increased; magistrates, judges, solicitors and barristers, social workers and probation officers all have a part to play in the formal response to repeated juvenile delinquency, especially when prison is a looming prospect.

The pattern of offending may also be little different from that described for the last episode, delinquency is still an occasional excursion. Indeed, this chapter has illustrated that the young people are more likely to heed societal rules. With greater planning and skill, the risk of a road traffic accident in a stolen car is reduced and, although crimes of violence are within reach, temptation is usually resisted. Nevertheless, the formal response to occasional findings of guilt is omnipresent. Almost every day of his life the offender will be reminded of his misdemeanours by probation officers, residential social workers, intermediate treatment officers or supervisors at an attendance centre or a community service scheme.

Moreover, it is possible to identify growing incongruity between the societal formal rules as laws are adapted to the needs of particular situations and individuals. Thus, as there is no fixed tariff of court disposals, the offender may experience different punishments for exactly the same crime. He may find that the police will be lenient or harsh when deciding on the severity of a charge or that they will ask the court to take some of his offences 'into consideration' when deciding on a sentence. This variable response will also be apparent from his social worker on whom he relies for a Social Enquiry Report. In a variety of circumstances the offender will find the societal rules applied differently.

Societal rules

1. Do not offend
2. Do not steal
3. Do not injure
4. Do not break into houses
5. Do not steal from cars
6. Do not take and drive away cars
7. Do not kill somebody when you steal a car
8. Do not break into a house when somebody is in the house
9. Feel guilty for the things you have done wrong
10. Feel that offending is unjust

Formal rules

1. If you offend you will be punished
2. If you offend more than three times you can expect to go to prison
3. Do not commit more serious crimes, for example, of violence
4. If you offend again you will go to prison
5. There is no fixed tariff of court disposals
6. Certain offences can be 'taken-into-consideration'
7. The severity of the charge will be decided by the police
8. A solicitor will help you with the court appearance
9. A social worker or probation officer will help you with your court appearance
10. A social worker or probation officer will prepare a Social Enquiry Report on your behalf

Belief rules

The young people present superficial explanations which suggest that they are helplessly pushed along the criminal road but, in fact, it requires careful negotiation. Persistent property offenders occasionally take a 'moral holiday' but they choose well-known destinations where the local customs and language present little difficulty. With each trip the young person becomes a little more experienced and skilled and develops rules which allow him to grasp opportunities during which expertise can be put to the test.

Over time, persistent delinquents begin to plan criminal excursions but, in the heady moments of the execution of the plan, the best designs go awry. Nonetheless, the subjects of this study are hardy souls, they are competitive and monadic, they harbour clear notions of territory and masculinity which and monadic, they harbour clear notions of territory and masculinity which means that they are not easily diverted from set goals. They possess rules of behaviour which allow them to enter into schemes which are doomed from the outset.

Belief rules

1. Use the crime to meet financial needs
2. Be assertive when offending
3. Be competitive
4. Offend in smaller numbers
5. Steal things which are easily sold
6. Learn how to sell the proceeds of your crime
7. Shop around to get a good price for the proceeds of crime
8. Glean the good things you experience as the result of a court disposal
9. Do not be concerned about experiences consequent upon a court disposal
10. Adopt short-term goals

Interaction rules

The repeated failure to avoid detection leads to placements in residential centres or a variety of community based schemes. During this time the persistent delinquent increasingly learns that it is best to co-operate with the statutory authorities and accept the consequences of his crime. He does what he is told when the solicitor advises him about pleas in court, he agrees with the magistrate who chastises him for being exceptionally naughty and dutifully promises never to do 'it' again. As one prisoner explained, 'these guys (the solicitors) have got it sewn up, so if they say look bad (guilty) you look bad.'

Although the young offender who continues with a criminal career becomes acquainted with many professional people and their clients, he is increasingly solitary as an offender. As evidence in this and the preceding chapter has shown, the persistent property offender becomes more aware of the benefits of working with those experienced in offending, who are trustworthy and will not 'grass you up', meaning to inform the police. Moreover, by reducing the number participating in the crime the returns -increasingly important during this episode- are increased. To repeat the words of a previous respondent, 'If you get 50 quid and there's one of you, you get 50 quid .... if there's six of you, you get fuck all.'

Nonetheless, the persistent property offender retains a reference group to whom he can boast about his criminal prowess or turn to for shelter from the more unpleasant aspects of the chosen life-style. Liaisons are difficult to maintain in a career which includes a variety of movements but the subjects of this study cling to one or two figures who share their values and beliefs.

However, what the young offender has to say about his delinquency is becoming increasingly out of tune with the experience of his home community. Indeed, the quotations used as illustrations in this chapter betray an argot and style better suited to an 'old lag', a persistent middle aged offender, well known to the custodial system. The terminology, such as 'at the end of my time', used by youngsters aged between fourteen and eighteen years are practically meaningless to the majority of adolescents. Other features of the persistent delinquent's life-style, offending alone and distinct social networks mean that it is always going to be difficult to convince local people that the chosen career route is viable.

Nonetheless, the 'audience' remains an integral part of persistent delinquency. Being caught requires repeated explanations for family and peers, the police and welfare agencies, court officials and magistrates. The rules to guide the young offender's interaction with these interested onlookers, which are listed below, are becoming increasingly incongruous with the rules that guide his criminal beliefs. The offender may say he feels helplessly pushed along a conveyor-belt to continued and more serious crime but he is now more assertive in his criminal behaviour and he uses a modicum of planning. Similarly, while he says that he does not intend to get convicted again, he knows that he will grasp the next good opportunity to steal that comes his way.

Interaction rules

1. Co-operate with the police
2. Co-operate with the solicitor
3. Co-operate with the court
4. Say that you will not get convicted again
5. Agree with the contents of the Social Enquiry Report
6. Say that your offending is getting worse and there is nothing you can do about it
7. Say that your placement in the CHE was great fun
8. Say that you found the detention centre no problem
9. Say that it's your social worker's fault that you are experiencing problems
10. Offend with somebody who knows what they are doing

Conclusions

How does the data collected in this chapter reflect upon the theoretical propositions about the criminal identity outlined in Chapter One? More evidence has been gathered which gives weight to the proposition that the criminal identity is based upon a series of decisions which appear rational to the offender. As the list of belief rules reveals, increasingly the rationale is the material gain to be reaped from the offence. However, as the career progresses, it takes upon a momentum of its own for, although the offender continues to choose his identity, he chooses from limited options.

Shared guidelines continue to play a part in the decision making but the young offender is becoming an increasingly solitary creature. He gains kudos from interaction with more law-abiding peers but this is becoming increasingly difficult. Indeed, respondents said they welcomed the opportunity to talk to friends about non-criminal matters! The offender now faces a dilemma because his identity has become divorced from his actual behaviour, what he says about crime seldom matches the rules he uses to guide his beliefs.

This is also a problem for the juvenile justice system earnestly trying to divert the young offender from his chosen life-style. The sentences of supervision, attendance centre and community service orders, local authority care with its residential component, each of these is re-interpreted by the offender and placed in a revised identity. Even the difficult negotiations with the police over findings of guilt, crimes to be taken-into-consideration or omitted from the charge sheet are taken in the adolescent offender's stride. The identity has clearly changed between the two episodes thus far described. It will be interesting to note further changes when the first days in prison are charted in the following pages. Will, for example, the young offender be able to subsume prison custody into his identity?

Summary Points

1. The young offender can present himself as helpless, demonstrating increasing criminality which he cannot control. Closer scrutiny shows that there is no pattern of increasing criminality, but that he drifts across crimes. Offenders take moral holidays but, over time, the destination becomes well known, less exciting and more predictable.
2. A modicum of planning is introduced into this holiday behaviour. However, for the excursion to take place, plans must coincide with opportunity and projects are often abandoned or bungled at the last minute.

3. In a subject matter which does not lend itself easily to aetiology, the disposition to commit an offence at some point in the future is a most important cause of crime.

4. The residents of the remand and the youth custody centre are very competitive and individualistic in their behaviour. They live from day-to-day using short-term goals hoping for better times to suddenly appear.

5. Adolescent gatherings provide a reference group to talk about crime, real or imaginary including a reference group for the criminal who wishes to get away from his crime.

6. Over time, the offender's patterns of association lead to networks for off-loading stolen goods which can subsequently precipitate criminal activity.

7. Persistent young offenders are herded together by the state, but their groups are regularly broken up by placement changes. Thus, inmates named long-standing acquaintances who followed a similar career as close friends.

8. When at liberty and offending, the sample population of this research know very well that detection and prosecution are likely. However, the past does little to deter as young offenders remember the pleasant aspects of previous placements, they seek patterns in their life experience and, in retrospect, life seems rosy.

9. Their relationship with statutory agencies varies; they respect those with power who are consistent, for example the police, they mistrust those with little power who are viewed as inconsistent, for instance, social workers.

10. The ten most prominent societal, formal, beliefs and interaction rules operating in this episode have been listed and discussed.

a) The societal rules have not changed but, given his greater skill in breaking the law, the offender is more likely to heed these publicly stated laws.

b) There is growing incongruity between societal and formal rules as laws are adapted to the needs of particular situations and individuals.

c) The belief rules used by the offenders in this episode reveal an increasingly ingrained criminal identity which allows the young person to enter into schemes which are doomed from the outset.

d) The interaction rules located in this episode reveal the variety of statutory agents to which he has been introduced. The offender promises to obey the law in the future but the interaction rules are becoming increasingly out of tune with his behaviour. The 'audience' remains an integral part of the behaviour.

8. First days in prison

This chapter returns to the episodes of the criminal career with a study of the young offender's first days in a penal institution. The 'formal system' imposed by those who organise the institution and its impact upon new entrants are described. Over time, the inmates begin to understand the 'informal system' developed by the residents of the institution. It is seen that these informal and formal systems are functional to the prison. In this context, the dynamics of prisoners' interaction are explored and a model in which conflict is minimised is put forward.

It has been seen that, although there are many routes into custody, the majority of young offenders who find their way into the penal system have kept in close touch with the police, courts and welfare agencies. Indeed, many of the young people have already had a taste of prison through a stay in a detention centre. Although they are only at the beginnings of their career, the study is suggesting that their relationship with the justice system will be long, enjoin considerable resource from the state and, for the recipients, it is likely to entail discomfort and deprivation.

This chapter begins with a brief description of the two institutions, a remand and a youth custody centre, participating in this study. The 'formal system', to borrow previous researchers' terms, is where the institution places constraints upon the inmates. But, as a comparison between official and inmates' versions of the daily routine demonstrates, the 'formal system' can be re-interpreted and subsumed into the 'informal system' constructed and maintained by the inmates. This acts as a valuable indicator of the ability of these young people to choose and maintain their own identity.

These processes are further explored by looking at hierarchies and groups within the prison setting. In Chapter Four, a view of hierarchy in closed settings was offered. This included leaders, lieutenants and a number of inmates excluded from the deviant group. In this chapter, a different explanation is put forward in which there is a place for everybody in the hierarchy. It is here that a clear view of the informal system emerges. The chapter concludes with a summary of the rules which underpin behaviour during the first days inside prison. Once again different patterns of congruence and correspondence between the different types of rule guiding different aspects of the offenders' behaviour are found.

The formal system

The data for this study were gathered in two institutions; a remand centre, for young prisoners under the age of 21 who await trial or sentence, and an open youth custody centre for young offenders sentenced for periods ranging between six and twenty-four months. These two prisons served quite different purposes and the settings differed markedly. However, certain similarities in the formal system imposed upon residents by the institutional routine become apparent upon close examination.

The youth custody centre was opened in 1948 in an old country mansion built by Bodley and Garner for the Earl of Plymouth in 1884. Bodley, who favoured the neo-Tudor for the court he designed for King's College Cambridge in 1893, preferred Jacobean for the stately home now housing young offenders. While King's has retained its role, status and most of its interior, the youth custody centre has experienced downward mobility and, stripped of its fixtures and fittings, it is reminiscent of a senior approved school where the inmates, 'display an unease about their tenure rather like squatters awaiting the return of homespun aristocrats' (Millham, Bullock and Cherrett 1975).

The remand centre was built in the extensive grounds of the youth custody centre in the 1960's as part of the expansion of specialized remand facilities. The remand centre has no Jacobean charm, it is a system of rectangular buildings surrounded by a thirty foot fence and elaborate security checks. One wing, formerly a high security nursery for pregnant female delinquents, now accommodates young offenders and other 'hard to place' inmates. In its exercise yard sits the now familiar portakabin, the education hut.

Both institutions are four miles away from two small dormitory towns which serve a large city. A visitor coming from this city endures forty minutes of bus and train rides followed by a twenty minute walk through the grounds of the old country estate as preparation for highly supervised contact with a loved one. In a number of respects, the remand and the youth custody centre are a long way from home.

The remand and the youth custody centres operate very similar regimes which closely mirror those for every other prison for young offenders in England and Wales. There is what some sociologists have called a formal order; for prisons this is laid down by the Home Office but will be adapted to meet local needs by the governor and his or her other staff. Of course, in this episode, the inmate is faced with a completely new set of what have been termed in this study 'formal' rules. What impact will these have upon his life?

Stripping the identity

The movement of a prisoner into a remand centre serves to exaggerate further the distance from home and family life. The young offender, at home one day, in the house of a stranger the same evening, caught and detained in police custody that night and remanded in custody the next day experiences a violent shift in identity. As one remandee elaborates,

> 'You get put into a van or, if there's a load of boys coming, you get put into a black Maria. You get taken here (the remand centre) you come into reception, you strip off, hand in your property, have a shower or bath, get changed into prison clothes. They mark you brown (not sentenced) or blue (not allocated) and you get put somewhere. You get put into 'C' wing first and then you get allocated to whatever block you are going to, 'D', 'A', or 'C'. That's it really. Then you just fall into line really.'

At this point in the process the institution, to use Goffman's (1961) term, 'strips' the prisoner of his identity and the prison exerts almost total control. The formal system is at its most powerful and the prisoner is virtually powerless. The inmate is disorientated, views through the meshed windows of the 'black Maria' provide few clues about the geographical setting of his destination. Even those in open youth custody centres, resident for over six months and aided by a stream of information, remain remarkably ignorant of the location of their temporary home, a factor which militates against successful escape should they try to abscond.

For some prisoners, the shock of a moving from liberty to security is acute. As one recent entry to the remand centre explains,

> 'Well I came to court on bail. They took my bail off me. I was on bail for 4 months. I went down from (the court) and went to the black Maria, came to the reception, told them a few things. Can't remember what I said now. And they gave me these prison clothes and put me on 'C' wing. They moved me to 'A' the next morning. I felt really sick....... The first week I didn't eat anything I just threw up all of it. And then I went to court and came back. And I thought this is it, this is it. This is the full stop. You're staying here. Then from that day it's OK. Take it the way it comes.'

Institutional routine

The institutions provide a routine which offers some comfort to prisoners who are unaware about where they are and what they are supposed to do. As the following description of a day in the life of a youth custody centre, which every trainee understands and should follow, there appears to be little room for manoeuvre.

'06.45 Lights on and rise; bed packs made up
07.00 Unlock applications, slop-out, wash and shave
07.30 Breakfast, back to cells, clean up and prepare for work
08.00 To work (overalls will be worn)
11.30 Cease work
11.40 Dinner, back to cells, prepare for work
13.30 To work (overalls must be worn)
16.30 Cease work
16.40 Tea, to cells
17.55 Unlock for classes
18.00 Unlock for association
20.00 Association ends, return to cells, slop out, supper
20.45 Night staff on duty
21.00 Day staff off duty'

In addition, prisoners must adhere to the prison regulations. The inmate does not carry with him, nor is he likely to see, a law-book. However, during the process of 'stripping' and early days of finding their feet, prisoners quickly acquire a full grasp of the essential laws. The following list was gleaned from a group of recent arrivals to both institutions.

'address staff by sir or name'
'bed packs made up daily'
'at adjudications inmates must be in best dress and slippers'
'at meals inmates have to be properly dressed in shoes and socks, and shirts inside their trousers'
'all items of kit are exchanged once a week and if any items are missing (the inmate is) placed on minor report'
'every Saturday morning one of the senior men like the Chief or the Governor or his Deputy inspects the landing.'

There are many rewards as well as sanctions which can be used to encourage the support of inmates for these laws and other aspects of the formal system. All prison settings are equipped with roles or jobs which offer a welcome change from a life in a cell or one part of the prison. Moreover, there can be status attached to particular jobs, for example the tea boy who has access to the kitchen and contraband. In particular, the education in the remand centre can provide warm relief from a stark atmosphere whilst certain types of employment in the youth custody centre are less arduous than others. These rewards are compounded by strict sanctions for persistent transgression of formal rules. These range from fines to being placed 'on the block', solitary confinement in a cell with the minimum of facilities.

'But when you get solitary confinement it's (the regime) different. You're in a (small) cell .... it's got like great big thick windows, mirrors, that you can't see through and it's got a load of shutters on the roof through which they can watch you.'

Interpreting the regime

The formal system and its accompanying rules are variously viewed as harsh, as is the prison setting and atmosphere, shocking, such as the move from police to prison custody, and like the prison laws, restricting. However, disadvantages are re-interpreted by the prisoner and extra emphasis is given to both the negative and positive features of prison life. For example, compare the routine previously described to that proffered by one who must adhere to its limits.

'Normal you get up. They come round about seven in the morning and bang on the door and tell you to get out of bed. And you get out of bed and get dressed and make your bedpack. About 15 minutes later they come and slop you out. Then have a wash, slop out, come back, sweep the cell out and then they lock you up. Then they come back and let you go for your breakfast. And then sometimes, not every day, about twice or three times a week they let you take exercise in the yard. That's only for 15 minutes. And then you go back. Back in your cell. Bang you up. Bang you up till half-ten and then they get you to scrub your cell out. And then they bang you up again and then about half-eleven you get dinner. And then they bang you up straight after dinner. Then sometimes they'll let you out to get to the Library. Half one-two o'clock and you might have association in the afternoon. Then they'll bang you up again before tea. They let you out for tea and then banged up again. Then you just stay inside until six o' clock. If it's your turn for association then you'll have it six till seven. But if it's not then you're there till morning. But if you've got association then you just mess around and then you've got supper. They just open the door, throw you some cakes and a cup of tea.'

These 'highlights' of the average day give a clear indication of the power of the formal system. However, the cold prison department terms are further cooled by prisoner terminology. The routine and argot belong to an older generation but the recipient and the speaker is only 16 years of age. Although inexperienced, he is already beginning to re-interpret and attach his own meaning to his situation.

It is possible for the offender to transgress the formal system and break publicly stated rules. Of course, most prisoners are well versed in the art of law-breaking and the attention of 'policemen' in a closed environment does little to deter. Indeed, with careful negotiation the prison officer can be lenient upon an inmate and turn a blind eye while minor laws are broken. As one young person explains,

> 'Some (laws) in here are bent, you know some (laws) are bent and some (laws) they keep to, they have to keep to. Like, they aren't allowed to give you fags or anything like that or dope, but they do give you fags and they do give you matches and lights away, so they are the (laws) they are bending. The (laws) that they don't bend are the kids wandering around on their own without telling, if the screws don't know where they are that's unprofessional and they could lose their jobs.'

The formal system is not fixed, it has its limits and these limits are constantly tested. Moreover, some of the flexibility in the formal system can be attributed to the actions of officers. As the research described in Chapter Four reveals, many studies consider prisoners and prison officers as homogeneous and conflicting groups. The evidence collected at the remand and youth custody centre dictates otherwise; prison officers differ markedly in personality and in their observance of the laws. As prisoners both benefit and suffer from the variable enforcement of the formal rules, their view of different officers will vary accordingly. For instance, one inmate observes,

> 'Some screws, they'll just get you to scrub your cell out and then they'll just go away again. And you just have a wander around. Most of them aren't like that. Mr. C. he'll just leave you alone while you do your cell. And others just say 'Come on'. But if you've got a bad one on 'bang-up' then you're a naughty boy and they don't like naughty boys.'

It can be seen that prisoners are very aware of the external controls that govern their life. They are both physically and emotionally distant from their home and 'normal' lifestyle. At the point of entry, there is a violent change of identity but there is an important institutional routine into which the prisoner must fit and a list of formal, publicly stated rules, many of which he must learn and, in the early stages, adhere to. Experienced inmates will discover which formal rules can be broken, which prison officers can be trusted and the limits imposed by the formal system are slowly pushed back. In the space that is created there develops an informal system, created and maintained by the residents, which is extremely pervasive.

Over time, the prisoner gets used to and adapts to the new regime but it would be a mistake to underestimate the unpleasantness of the prisoners' predicament, especially for the young who share the closed setting of a remand centre and who remain unsure about their length of stay in the institution. Remand prisoners share different types of cell unless they are 'on the block', a single room with no windows and a peep-hole in the ceiling. The most common cell accommodates four in two bunk beds and is some four metres square. It has a grey tiled floor and painted concrete walls, decorated with a little graffiti or a chiselled message from a recent resident. On one wall there is a light switch and alarm bell, on the opposite wall a bare notice board. The door to the cells are metal, covered in graffiti punctuated only by a thin sliver of 'plastic glass'. The fourth wall holds the barred window above a boiling-hot radiator.

The window boasts a most depressing view and admits a singularly dreadful smell. Standing on the radiator and looking through the bars residents are met with the steamy redolence of urine evacuated out of the cell window the night before. The grass below is littered with envelopes of faeces thrown from the room, usually with some gusto if the contents are not to be traced to their owner. Given staff shortages it is not always possible for inmates to go to the toilet at night and posting excrement out of the window is often preferred to leaving it to mature in a pot until slopping out time. Through the haze, prisoners view a ten metre fence topped with barbed wire, beyond the fence there is a wood and beyond the wood there is a fading world of liberty and potential crime. For the prisoner, the formal system leaves a lot to be desired and any alternative constructed by the inmates will have many instant supporters.

Developing an informal system

Prisoners in remand and youth custody centres showed a consistent ability to conquer the less savoury aspects of their existence. The crucial part of this process is the ability to develop consensus and order internal to and constructed by the group. Such tenor may be more perceived than real, but it plays an important part in prison life.

The literature dealing with institutional life emphasises the hierarchical nature of inmate groups with leaders, lieutenants and followers. In this model, bad prisoners inside the group can be clearly distinguished from the good prisoners outside of it. Moreover, descriptions of the informal social system focus upon its conflict with wider societal norms. A cursory glance at interaction within the remand and youth custody centre can lead observers to the mistaken belief that such a structure still exists. For example, youth custody boys noted that

> 'R____ is the daddy of this place, he's the one (prisoner) who counts, who says what is and isn't on.'

But, closer and more detailed study reveals a more complicated picture where all prisoners make a positive contribution. As the previous chapter has shown, most inmates arrive at the remand or youth custody centre with a previous criminal and/or institutional background and this experience is a useful entree to prison life. New arrivals are generally well versed in behaviour patterns which set them apart from others of their own age. The prison setting brings together a group of people of a similar experience but, nonetheless, patterns of hesitant negotiation persist as the inmate looks for two or three others upon whom he can rely and trust. One remandee explains,

> 'Oh well, when you come in here you just know you can't trust no-one 'cos, right, it's like being outside, you know, you can't rely on no-one. You get on with people, right, you get on with people in a certain respect, but you can't trust them often because they'll rob you and things like that. But you do get proper kids in here and you know where you stand with them, but I had to find that out. I knew sort of vaguely that I couldn't trust no-one from experience, but you have to find out what the crack is, you've got to get into the routine first, people have to see what the crack is.'

Another prisoner elaborates on the difference between one view of prison life which emphasises the leader and his followers and another, which must accommodate the necessities of everyday living.

> 'Well people talk about 'Daddies' (leaders) and all that but most of it is just a load of shit really. Like I know up the other end (of the youth custody centre) they talk about G____ who will fight with anyone. But that's nothing to do with me. I'm here for another six months and we all just want to get on with it. I know I've got a couple of mates I can rely upon, if necessary, and I can look after myself. But I'll get on with everybody, you've just got to get on with it and have a laugh and that.'

As another prisoner explains, in this episode the inmates are anxious to keep their self-respect and make the most of a poor situation.

> 'You've got to make the most of what you can and keep your head up. You've got to keep your eye on others who know what they're doing and work out

what's going on. And you can make things much better for yourself. You can get some work in the kitchens. You can go to the library, you can even go to classes. Like, you don't want to work and you probably can't read but it gets you out and about doesn't it? You've got to play the system.'

Movement of prisoners

In the youth custody centre, where inmates may stay for relatively long periods of time, stable relationships are feasible. However, in the remand centre, inmates will leave the wing once a week for a court appearance and return is not guaranteed. In this scheme, those who do return find themselves allocated to new cells and, consequently, meet new associates.

Table 8.1: Number of cell moves by remand prisoners
over a nine day period

Cell Moves	%
0	25
1	15
2	20
3	10
4	20
5	10
	(N=20)

Total moves: 43 (mean per prisoner = 2.15)

In order to gauge the frequency of movement within the remand centre, it was decided to trace the movement of twenty prisoners over a short period of nine working days during the first period of fieldwork. As the previous table illustrates, changing cell is frequent, as two-thirds of inmates move at least twice in a few days.

Over the nine-day period, eighty young people were placed in 26 functioning cells on the remand centre wing. All bar nine of the cells are shared by two to four remandees and five 'dormitory' rooms cater for five or more prisoners. Thus, most inmates find themselves placed in intimate contact with two or more others for long periods of the day. However, frequent re-allocation means that close partners often change and, indeed, the analysis of prison movement reveals that, on average, each inmate shares a cell with five (5.4) others over the nine-day period and that whilst two remandees were alone for the entire period of study, two others came into close contact with 14 others who differed markedly in their presenting personalities and offence histories. As one young person remanded to custody remarked, 'you're always on the go in this place, you're sleeping with somebody new each night.'

In the youth custody centre, those not living on the punishment wing were allocated to sixteen dormitories sleeping between five and twelve young people. The age, type of offence and geographical location of the trainees' home were scrutinized for all inmates living in the youth custody centre and no common patterns emerged. Each dormitory consisted of young offenders across a relatively wide age range, with different offence histories and dissimilar geographical backgrounds.

This evidence suggests that movement of prisoners and subsequent patterns of interaction is integral to the informal system. Initially, it can be seen that prisoners bring to the institution some knowledge of residential centres and some will be acquainted with other residents. Nevertheless, the first days of their stay in a new setting will be spent in a state of mistrust seeking two or three other reliable companions. Despite the cell system in the remand centre, contacts with other prisoners will be frequent and a network of associates quickly develops. Having established this mortise, it is possible further to scrutinize inmates' interaction and to discover whether streaming takes place and whether prisoners attempt to regularize patterns of contact to take account of types of offending and personality.

Hierarchies and groups

It will be recalled from Chapter Four that on the football terrace Marsh (1978) was able to locate three specific groups amongst football fans, 'rowdies', 'nutters' and 'novices' who assumed different patterns of behaviour within a common scheme of hooliganism. As the review of prison research illustrated, there are many identities available to the adult prisoner, for example Schrag's (1954) 'right guys' or Irwin's (1970) 'gleaners'. Moreover, Giallombardo (1966) has taught us that prisoners assume different roles at different stages in the sentence. In the remand and the youth custody centre some prisoners were able to distinguish between the identity assumed by their fellow inmates. For example, one prisoner remarks,

'Say there are three levels; nutters, they just don't care, they tell the screws to fuck off, you know, start fighting with the screws; the kids that can look after themselves in the middle, they just have a laugh and act normal and can look after themselves if necessary; the wankers are at the bottom, the smaller kids, the mouthy kids (boasting), the bent kids (homosexuality), the rapists, just people who aren't going to defend themselves, you know?'

However, this pattern does not sustain over a number of interviews. It will be seen that some of the characteristics of prisoners at the bottom of this hierarchy, for example homosexuality and a tendency to exaggerate are, in fact, common to prison life. Moreover, associations between prisoners revealed in the interviews are short-lived and inmates who were 'outside' of a group suddenly become integral members. For example,

'I hang about, there's about six or seven of us and we have a good laugh, but we don't cause trouble, we leave that to another group on the wing. There's a little mob who try to think they're hard (tough) and they set that kid on fire.....I mean that kid was sitting on his own, he don't talk to nobody and they went and set him on fire. But now he's talking to us, you know, so things are much better for him.'

This evidence runs counter to findings of other researchers that clear and fixed hierarchies dominate penal institutions. In order further to explore this area it was decided to mount a small sub-study of the dynamics of inmate groups. During research in the remand centre, twenty-five prisoners who had previously been interviewed individually were interviewed in five groups of five. The groups were assembled in accordance with the order of interviews and disregarded the friendship pattern of the prisoners. Nevertheless, each prisoner knew the others in his group.

The transcripts of the five group interviews were then analysed using group dynamics techniques. The analysis concentrated upon the first two hundred utterances in four subject areas to be discussed during the interview. Despite the fact that conversations took place in the presence of an interviewer, these data point towards some interesting findings concerning prisoner interaction.

Initially, it was found that within each group of prisoners, two inmates make a far greater contribution than the other three. As the following table illustrates, on average the two principal characters made three-fifths of the contributions. However, it will also be noted that the most frequent contributor hardly dominated the group, indeed the highest recorded proportion of utterances from one person was 38% (Group E).

Table 8.2: The proportion of utterances contributed by each group member in one subject area in five groups

Group Member	Group					
	A	B	C	D	E	Total
	%	%	%	%	%	%
1	32	29	32	30	38	32 ⎫
						⎬ 60
2	31	28	30	22	28	28 ⎭
3	16	20	18	21	15	18 ⎫
4	15	18	18	18	13	16 ⎬ 40
5	6	5	2	9	6	6 ⎭
	(N=182)	(N=198)	(N=188)	(N=190)	(N=190)	(N=948)

Although it was difficult to chart exact patterns in a small number of groups, there appeared to be no relationship between the propensity to contribute and the age, offence, previous institutional history, length of stay or physical size (height) of the prisoner.

Thus, in conversation about prison life and offending, no one inmate dominated the conversation in all groups and none of the participants was excluded from the discussion. Moreover, when this analysis is applied to particular subject areas within each group, it can be seen that there is considerable variation around the norm. As the following table illustrates, some members of the group can be very authoritative about particular subjects but less forthcoming about others. For example, within Group A, two-fifths (39%) of the conversation devoted to the subject of burglary belongs to contributor 2, but he is much less authoritative on the question of prison officers (24%). Contributor 5, on the other hand, reserved almost half of his offerings for the subject of burglary.

**Table 8.3: Number of contributions to the conversation
cross-tabulated by subject area (Group A)**

| | Contributor | | | | | |
Subject	1	2	3	4	5	Total
Racism	N=60	N=64	N=29	N=36	N=7	N=196
Prison Officers	65	48	44	30	13	200
Burglary	55	77	30	13	25	200
Other Prisoners	75	55	20	40	10	200
TOTAL	255	244	123	119	55	796

This evidence further questions the literature which suggests that prisoner groups have strong leaders who dominate, followers who are subservient and outsiders who are excluded.

The contributions made by Group A in the four subject areas of Racism, Prison Officers, Burglary and Other Prisoners have also been analysed using the techniques developed by Bales (1950). Each offering is categorized into twelve areas which reveal something of the nature of each utterance, if it is positive or negative, whether it attempts to answer problems posed to the group or raises further questions and, possibly, tension. The results of this analysis, laid out in the following table 8.4, clearly demonstrate that there is little disagreement within the group, indeed there appears to be a great deal of co-operation.

Two-thirds of all utterances were attempted answers to questions posed by other group members. Most of this category of contributions was concerned with giving orientation, that is repeating and clarifying certain points. A further 15 per cent of all responses were categorized as positive, the great majority of which were expressions of agreement, understanding and concurrence with the points made by other group members. Only a very small proportion (5%) of contributions made by group members could be categorized as 'negative reactions' and there were no displays of antagonism.

This evidence on the dynamics of prisoner groups reveals that, contrary to the rigid hierarchical perspective adopted by much of the penological literature, more negotiation appears to be taking place. In conversation, inmates are able to make varying levels of input according to the subject under discussion.

Table 8.4: Group dynamics within Group A using techniques developed by Bales (1950)

Type of Response	%
Shows solidarity	0.6
Shows tension release	0.3
Agrees	13.9
Positive reactions	*14.8*
Gives suggestion	0.1
Gives opinion	26.1
Gives orientation	47.0
Attempted answers	*73.2*
Asks for orientation	5.9
Asks for opinion	0.8
Asks for suggestion	0.3
Questions	*6.9*
Disagrees	0.6
Shows tension	4.4
Shows antagonism	0
negatives answers	*5.0*
	(N=796)

Let us now turn to the rules which operate in this episode of the criminal career.

Rules of behaviour

In this chapter, specific aspects of the first few days that young property offenders spend in penal custody have been highlighted. The institutional routine imposed as part of the formal system has been described together with the informal system created and maintained by the residents of the remand and the youth custody centre. The movement and group dynamics of prisoners have also been scrutinised. What does this evidence tell us about the rules which underpin the behaviour of the subjects under study and how will they help us to understand the criminal identity? Once again, the societal, formal, belief and interaction rules operating in this episode are discussed.

Societal rules

The societal rules operating in this episode do not differ from those described earlier. However, because of the offender's situation some cannot apply, for example breaking into a house or stealing a car are presumably remote possibilities when the inmate is locked up. Other rules do apply; theft is as likely in prison as elsewhere and reminders to the prisoner that he has 'done wrong' and acted in an unjust way will be ever present. But the shock of entry into the institution is likely to make any consideration of these rules on the part of the prisoner unlikely. Indeed, it is very difficult for the inmate to connect his current predicament with his previous behaviour.

Societal rules

1. Do not offend
2. Do not steal
3. Do not injure
4. Do not break into houses
5. Do not steal from cars
6. Do not take and drive away cars
7. Do not kill somebody when you steal a car
8. Do not break into a house when somebody is in the house
9. Feel guilty about the things you have done wrong
10. Feel that offending is unjust.

Formal rules and Interaction rules

In this episode of the criminal career, formal rules dominate the inmate's behaviour. In his first days in prison, the young prisoner has to conform to the collocation that characterises residential life. The motivation that led the offender to break the law has gone. During the first days on remand, inmates are very disorientated and find themselves powerless to challenge the laws that make the regime tick over. Thus, there are a series of interaction rules about conforming to the institutional routine and during the period following the first reception to prison no sanctions are needed to enforce these rules.

The ambiance within which the formal system operates differs markedly between the maximum security remand centre and the youth custody centre operating from a redundant country mansion. Nonetheless, in either setting, the first days can be extremely distressing and formal rules can be instrumental in helping the inmate to cope with his situation. This chapter has described how young offenders are whisked from liberty to security with little idea about their geographical setting and they feel emotionally distant from home. They are 'stripped' of certain facets of their identity and placed in conditions which can best be described as extremely unpleasant. Indeed, a number of respondents, including one quoted in this chapter, explained that they felt physically ill during their first days in prison. Moreover, it should not be forgotten that the prisoner has had his freedom curtailed.

It is clear that the new entrant has to deal with many problems and there is a high premium on rules which ease the transition from 'citizen' to 'prisoner'. There is flexibility in the formal system as officers allow certain minor rules to be broken or bent. By offering an inmate a cigarette or a match, allowing him to make a token effort at the daily scrubbing of the floor or simply having a chat with him about a subject other than the institutional regime, the prison officer adds some warmth to an otherwise cold existence. One prisoner illustrates this point when he says,

> 'You might get caught with a bit of tobacco, right, and some officers might say it's your hard luck and put you on report but others will just turn a blind eye and forget it like, you've got to work out who's who.'

The list of rules which the prisoner uses to guide his interaction in the prison is almost exactly the same as the formal rules just described. No matter how the prisoner feels about his predicament, and it has been seen that the institution can bring about physical sickness as well as emotional imbalance, he will find that it is best to do exactly as he is told, to wear prison uniform, to go to the cell he is allocated to, to get up, eat and sleep when he is told.

The placement also brings the young offender into contact with a stream of new faces each of which expresses varying degrees of knowledge about the regime. At first these friendly souls are not always a welcome sight as the prisoner is never sure who is going to steal from him, bully him or generally give him a hard time. One prisoner noted that, 'you can't trust nobody in this place, if you drop off (report to prison officers) on your mates you'll drop off on your granny but most of them in here wouldn't think twice about dropping off on their granny.' The inmates enter into hesitant patterns of negotiation as they find two or three others who can be relied upon. In the remand centre, this is a never-ending quest as there is frequent movement in, out and around the institution. There are no dominant groups and those excluded from a particular assembly can soon become an integral member. Prisoners learn to 'give and take', in assembly with each other. In institutions where the incarcerated can be locked up in small groups for 23 hours at a time, co-operation and flexibility in behaviour patterns are the order of the day.

The following list of rules has been extrapolated from the interviews with prisoners; indeed, most are identifiable in the quotations used as illustrations in this chapter.

Formal rules

1. Remand prisoners will wear different colours depending upon whether they are sentenced or unallocated.
2. Young remand prisoners will be placed separately from older prisoners
3. Prisoners convicted or charged with grave crimes will be placed with the older prisoners
4. Prisoners will follow a strict regime
5. Prisoners will rise at 06.45
6. Prisoners to make up bed-packs
7. Prisoners to slop out, wash and shave every morning
8. Prisoners to return to cells after breakfast
9. Prisoners to work 08.00 to 11.30
10. Prisoners to have dinner back at cells

Interaction rules

1. Follow the prison regime (as in formal rules)
2. Do exactly as you are told
3. Take any jobs on offer
4. Agree with the prison officer
5. Take any educational course on offer
6. Take trips to the library
7. Do not be seen to be involved in any trouble
8. Begin to enjoy the company of other prisoners
9. Say that you know what you are doing
10. Say that you know what is expected of you

Belief rules

Although there is now a deal of harmony between the formal rules of the institution and the interaction rules of the prisoner, there is no evidence to suggest that the inmate changes his belief rules. In his interaction he follows the institutional regime, does as he is told, becomes involved in vocational exercises and appears to know what he is doing. The interview transcripts also reveal that the inmate never feels he can rely upon anybody during his first days in the prison and that he will be extremely careful in taking his time to work out whom he can trust, a technique that may be learned from previous stays in residential care. Whilst the inmate is lumped together in prison with other inmates he will attempt to emphasise his independence and to distinguish between and attach status to other criminals. The disjunction, during the early days in prison, between the private and public self is considerable.

Belief rules

1. Do not rely upon anybody
2. Take your time working out whom you can trust
3. Be especially wary of prison officers
4. Be careful that other inmates do not steal from you
5. Work out the institutional regime
6. Work out how experienced prisoners work the system
7. Keep your head down and do your time
8. Emphasise your independence
9. Begin to distinguish between and attach status to other groups of prisoners
10. Do not say where you have come from or what you have done

Conclusions

In this episode there has been a radical change in both the situation of the young people being studied and the rules which guide their behaviour. How has this reflected upon their criminal identity which, until the violent upheaval of being placed in a penal institution, was progressing smoothly? To answer this question, the theoretical propositions outlined in Chapter One will be re-examined in the light of the evidence just presented.

Does the inmate choose his identity on the basis of a series of decisions which seem rational to him? In this episode the inmate has little choice about many decisions, he must follow the institutional regime and do as he is told or face harsh penalties which can include solitary confinement. However, the prisoners show no resistance to formal rules during the days following reception to prison and, indeed, anxious to demonstrate that he is unconcerned and that he knows what he is doing, the inmate welcomes clear guidelines to follow.

In this episode the formal rules differ little from those the inmate uses to guide his interaction as a prisoner. Thus at this stage in the career, whilst the response of the justice system to juvenile offending, a spell of prison custody, does not reinforce the criminal identity, it is certainly crucial in guiding inmates' action. However, over time, once recovered from the shock of incarceration, the prisoner begins to rebuild his confidence and to incorporate the formal rules into a revised identity. This change is surely inevitable for, although the formal system dominates the inmate's existence for the first few days, the formal rules could not be maintained on the basis of the rewards and sanctions available to dissuade inmates from going against the grain. The institutions are only viable if the formal rules are adhered to and it will be interesting in the coming chapter to see how the relationship between the formal and informal system develops.

Shared guidelines are certainly operating during the prisoner's stay in prison. The analysis of group dynamics reveals how prisoners show co-operation and flexibility but do not display antagonism or solidarity. Perhaps this is an expected response, particularly amongst inmates who are locked up with two or three others in a cell for 23 hours a day. Again, it will be interesting to see in the next episode how the inmate's identity develops during these long periods in one another's company.

It is particularly noteworthy that the inmate's presentation of self is partial in this episode for it excludes great chunks of their past. New arrivals do not talk about how they got to prison or the offence that precipitated their arrival. However, whenever possible, the inmates continue to present as confident and in control. Indeed, the rules that guide the inmate's interaction are becoming increasingly incongruous with the belief rules. The behaviour is routine and consequent upon the inmate's powerlessness to challenge the formal system, yet the identity exudes the confidence of one who is in control of his destiny. The criminal identity has clearly changed during this episode. Let us see if there are further developments in the final episode to be looked at in this study.

Summary Points

1. The remand and the youth custody centre operate from very different settings. Both penal establishments are distant, both physically and emotionally, from the inmate's home.
2. This distance is further exaggerated by the movement from home to custody and during the process of 'stripping', the institution exerts almost total control.

3. The prison laws and routine can provide comfort for the recipient, but it is also recognized that the setting is harsh, shocking and restricting.

4. Young offenders adapt to and re-interpret the regime. They adopt the argot of an older generation. They find that prison officers will be lenient as well as harsh and, gradually the informal social system becomes as pervasive as the formal system.

5. Most prisoners arrive with a previous experience of residential care. This breeds mistrust and new entrants are hesitant as they seek out two or three others on whom they can rely.

6. The patterns of movement within the remand centre and physical make-up of the youth custody centre mean that each inmate meets a lot of people. Generally, inmates do their best to accommodate one another.

7. The evidence does not suggest hierarchies of domination with fixed leaders. Hierarchies exist, but different prisoners take dominant roles in alternate situations and all make a contribution. Analysis of the dynamics of inmate groups provides further evidence of co-operation between prisoners.

8. The ten most prominent societal, formal belief and interaction rules operating in this episode have been listed and described.

a) A number of societal rules no longer apply to the incarcerated offender. However, all those which are applicable to prison will be followed by the inmate who is somewhat shell-shocked by his entry to custody.

b) During their first few days in prison, inmates feel disorientated and are powerless to challenge the formal rules that make the regime work. Flexibility in formal rules aids the transition from citizen to prisoner and is welcomed by the inmates.

c) Although the inmates may follow the formal rules of the institution there is no evidence to suggest that his belief rules have changed at all.

d) The interaction rules stress the need to concur with prison officers' commands and take extreme care in interaction with inmates.

9. Established in prison

This chapter focuses upon the adaptations of prisoners who have overcome the shock of moving from liberty to security and who envisage relatively long stays in custody. The inmate's presentation of his situation and the sanctions which help to maintain the increasingly important informal system are examined. The relationship between different types of prisoner and the impact of custody after discharge are studied.

In the last chapter, it was seen that the first days in a remand or youth custody centre are shocking to the participants. But as they settle into their routine, adapt to the formal system and contribute to the informal system, how do young prisoners cope with their continuing deprived existence? In previous chapters charting progress before remand or sentence to custody, individuality and competitiveness characterised the offender's life, how are these emotions channelled in an environment that requires co-operation for its viability? What are the sanctions used by inmates in the maintenance of the informal system? In this penultimate chapter, as part of the analysis of the continuing criminal identity, these questions are addressed.

This chapter will also discuss the contribution of different types of criminal to institutional life and the benefits they are able to glean from a seemingly barren setting. The study is principally concerned with young property offenders, the most common grouping in remand and youth custody centres. However, these offenders also enjoy a relationship with those convicted of more serious crimes, for example murderers and rapists, whom they will meet as part of custodial life. Generally, offenders mix together and, as the evidence demonstrates, inmates spend considerable time talking about crime.

A feature of life which was particularly important in the first episode to be scrutinized in this study re-appears in this chapter. Prisoners spend an inordinate amount of time 'doing nothing' and during this time delinquent techniques are gleaned from one another. There will be other features of the custodial experience which will stick with the prisoner after release. What then are his expectations of the future? As we shall see, inmates -even at this tender age- have little expectation of 'going straight' and, locked into a specific career, only the optimists see escape routes in pipe dreams of never getting caught or, even more unlikely, 'pulling off the big job'.

Let us begin by looking at the prisoner's presentation of self.

Prisoner's presentation of self

As evidence on young offenders' experience of residential care has shown, the participants in this study are capable of re-negotiating their predicament and making difficult situations appear acceptable. Observation and interviews with the prisoners suggest that, over time, this process is also a feature of prison life as inmates develop a façade which hides many of the unpleasant aspects of prison life. This translation of events is key to the maintenance of the criminal identity.

For example, although initially reticent, once they regain their confidence, residents of the remand and the youth custody centre eagerly exaggerate stories told to one another and easily adopt prison mythology; ideas about adult prisons which have been picked up on the way through the system. As the quotations used to illustrate the evidence in the following pages demonstrate, prisoners will emphasise their machismo, independence and heterosexual prowess in descriptions and justification of their offending patterns. This usually involves a good deal of criminal argot.

However, the formal system and its accompanying rules remain very pervasive. Although the inmate quickly becomes aware of what is expected of him and adapts to the institutional regime, he cannot escape it. The same dreadful conditions in the remand centre which were described in the previous chapter persist. Nonetheless, in their conversation they cover reality with an attractive veneer which bears little relationship to their actual predicament. To instance the difference between the reality and the image two examples are available. The first concerns the prisoner's sexuality, the second highlights the inmates' treatment of sex offenders.

When prisoners discuss with each other their sexuality, it is girlfriends and occasionally wives who feature. Letters and, more importantly, visits from girlfriends soon become public knowledge and are treasured by prisoners as symbols of their masculinity. However, the actual interaction with loved ones during a visit is usually strained and lingering embraces across the visiting table tend to be for the benefit of other prisoners and visitors. But when the girlfriends are reminiscing on the long bus journey home, the boys return to an environment in which heterosexual relationships are almost absent. Indeed, homosexuality is relatively common, yet is never openly discussed among prisoners. A prison officer sums up the situation thus;

'They are prolific liars in here (youth custody centre). They've all got Jag's, no-one's got a Mini. Wouldn't you fantasize if you were in that state? It's only natural I suppose..... I suppose homosexuality is normal to prisons, it's only natural. If you're going to deprive somebody of something you're bound to get some kind of perversion aren't you? Why do people hold their hands up in shame? They are aghast with shock when it happens. It's stupid...... I mean they aren't a bunch of queers or rampant homosexuals or anything or child molesters.'

The second example of the disjunction between prisoners' descriptions of their situation and their actual behaviour is apparent in the treatment of others charged with or found guilty of offences of a sexual nature. It is well known that rapists or child-murderers are often isolated in adult prisons to protect them from physical intimidation from other inmates. In describing their current situation, young prisoners often attempt to re-create those aspects of the adult institution. Consequently, the following type of quotation was common in the remand centre.

'The screws just drop the hint. You know, 'fuckin' hell, look at what he's up for, 12 rapes of young girls', you know. 'What's his name? M_____, M_____, Oh, M_____, that's right', you know in the black Maria or something on the way down, the word would go round and that kid would get fucked (beaten) up.'

But, as evidence from the previous chapter has shown, there is no exclusion of particular types of criminal from cohesive groups. Indeed, observation and further interviews with inmates revealed that there is no rounding upon young offenders because of their crime. Moreover, twenty year old rapists and murderers in the remand centre are placed on the wing reserved for offenders aged 18 years or less for their own safety. This would seem to suggest that informal rules regarding certain types of criminals are exercised amongst groups of 18-21 year olds, but not amongst the younger prisoners.

However, the talk and exaggeration common in the claims of the less experienced resident are functional in the sense that they conceal some of the tedium of prison life and provide more dimensions to an otherwise limited existence. As Cohen and Taylor (1981) found in their research at Durham Prison, minor events become life-and-death issues in a closed environment and the remand and the youth custody centre are no exceptions to this rule. For example, single events reverberated around the wing of the remand centre for many days. There follows a description of an unusual event during the period of fieldwork.

'Well, I threw this tray at the kitchen boy and this screw (prison officer) and another screw grabbed me and put his arm round my throat and started strangling me. So I said 'Ok I'll walk' and he wouldn't let me go so I shouted to him 'Ok I'll fuckin' walk' and then he pointed towards me. So I went to hit him, right, and it was only because he was holding me that I went to hit him. And this screw came in and he marched me down to the cell. And still he had his arm around me and for about 10 minutes after, and then they started hitting me. They don't hit you in front of the kids.'

This story was recounted in various forms by ten young people interviewed during the following three days and by two young people a week later when the inmate involved in the dispute had left the prison. The validity of the story is doubtful but it does show how particular events suitably embroidered can brighten up a tedious life. It is also noteworthy that the conflict of the event is maximised although, as the following pages reveal, actual violence between prisoners is rare.

It is perhaps surprising that more conflict in prisons is not found. Inmates have transgressed the rule of law, they have been labelled as deviant by society and they carry the stigma of a court appearance and a custodial sentence. Their life chances are practically nil. However, within the prison situation there is no flight to hedonism and there is relatively little disorder. Indeed, most of the prisoner's energy is channelled into the maintenance of the informal system, for prisoners who have recovered from the shock of incarceration and who expect relatively long periods of detention have little else to do. For example, witness the sanctions used by residents to make sure that the informal rules of behaviour are followed.

Informal sanctions

It is clear that there are strong formal controls in prisons which are maintained by strict sanctions. This chapter has recounted the development of informal rules which inmates use, principally to divert their attention from their dire predicament. Indeed, the formal system, together with the informal system developed and maintained by residents, set limits upon prisoners' behaviour. There are also penalties imposed upon those who upset the informal system, only these are cruder than their formal counterparts. The principal form of sanction is through physical violence or the threat of physical violence.

The evidence collected for this study suggests that aggression or fighting are seldom spontaneous amongst prisoners in the remand centre and the youth custody centre; it is usually arranged. Further, a fight rarely involves more than two combatants, although it will usually draw an audience. There is little physical violence involved and the whole event seldom lasts more than a minute. Prison officers, the source of formal control, are usually excluded and only invited to intervene if the fight goes beyond limits acceptable to the inmates.

For example, one prisoner, asked to explain what happens in the event of an impasse between two prisoners, suggests the following scenario is very probable.

'Oh well they just say, 'See you in the bogs tonight'. If they are in there then one kid will keep a look out, then one kid will say, 'Well do you want to mouth it then do ya' (meaning, you still want to say what you were saying about me). Then you will just start fighting. You know a kid will keep watch until a screw comes in, then he will call 'screw', then the fight will stop.'

Prison officers report that most fights do not result in much, if any, physical injury to the participants. They do not see it as anything out of the ordinary or as a serious occurrence. However, for those cases they do come across, they will put a well-tried procedure into operation. A prison officer elaborates.

'There were two boys this morning who had a punch-up in the kitchen. I'll just see that there's no serious damage to them, what was the reason, and possibly one of them or both will be put on governor's report. ...... But if one of them has a black eye or something like that, then there might be an investigation.'

But fights rarely involve anything as serious as a black eye; indeed the language prisoners use to describe the event seems to be the most violent component of the affair!

'Well, I had a kid in my cell who went to court today who was going 'all my people round my area are harder than your people'. So I walked away from it twice and he offered me out (asked me to fight) twice. And then he nicked my matches, so I agreed to see him later (for a fight). So I smacked the shit out of him good style. He didn't nick my matches again.'

In their keenness to manufacture competition and opposition, prisoners can make fiction triumph over fact and the remand and the youth custody centre begin to resemble North American prisons earlier described. However, as the interviews with young prisoners lengthened, so the stories of violence and aggression become quiescent. Surely prisoners can become involved in fights, sometimes over trivial matters such as a football team. For example, during the period of fieldwork, one remandee attacked another who had the name of his home town tattooed on his neck. When asked why the fight occurred, the aggressor reasoned that lads from his geographical area must always stand up for themselves, a reminder of the territorial awareness commented upon earlier.

'You get fights as well over trivial things like who supports what football team. (laughs). Things like that. I knew a kid who had a fight with a kid in from W_____. He had 'W_____' tattooed on his neck. He did it 'cos he was from C_____'.

But, for a group of young people who include violent criminals amongst their number, life is relatively tranquil and aggression is not central to their prison life. It is however an important option in resolving disputes and the real key to its success as a piece of behaviour is that neither participant needs to win; they simply need to take part, to display their willingness to defend their corner. For most disputes are not, of course, life-and-death matters and whilst the name of your home town emblazoned on your neck can assume great importance to other prisoners, its ceases to be of any significance once the dispute is resolved. Thus, a common description of the ending of a fight sequence was,

'The next day they're the best of fuckin' mates you know, talking to each other. You know they've got all their differences worked out, you know, that's it.'

Moreover, in many instances, it seems that disputes between prisoners appear to be resolved without the effort of resorting to a fight. The highly symbolic event is simply acknowledged to have taken place. Thus a prisoner in the youth custody centre reports:

'I am more or less the same size as, say, Brian. Then we can tell just by looking at each other, we know we don't fuck (fight) with each other. There's no point to it.'

Clearly, the environment in which prisoners find themselves demands co-operation and understanding, a demand which can be difficult to meet given the characteristics and previously described identity of the residents. As the following two respondents report, the informal system reaches an understanding with the formal system.

'You've got to survive in here. You've got to mind your own business, have a good laugh, don't be a pad (cell) thief, don't be cheeky to staff, don't mouth it (brag) .... all of these things, but we all do these things so, sometimes, you have to stand up for yourself and get things sorted out.'

''course, there's all kinds of things going on against the (formal) rules, baroning, like giving a kid a fag (cigarette) if he gives you two back, canteening, that's if you're out (of prison) and I'm in and you give me something to give somebody else. So, you've got all this going on and you have to watch out for yourself, nobody is here to do you any favours.'

This evidence is most illuminating. It has been seen that persistent young offenders can be solitary in their criminal activity but competitive in their more gregarious moments. Adapting to the wants of others can require great sacrifice for all members of society, but young prisoners, who live in very close confines, find special and individual difficulties. There is a need to survive in a harsh environment with others who are not friends by choice. The fights which form the principal sanction in maintaining the informal system and the violence and aggression which characterise their descriptions form useful vehicles into which conflict can be channelled. The inmates are competitive but they manage to maintain rivalries in a co-operative atmosphere. As one remandee illustrates, a compromise is reached,

'Everybody sticks together really, but we might stick together but half of us hate each other, do you know what I mean? Like I don't like half the kids in here and I don't think they like me.'

The contribution of different prisoners

There is a tendency for observers of prison life to categorize inmates according to their crime, its type, severity or nature. For those who are part of the culture, however, criminal history is less important and, in the pursuit of an orderly society, it is necessary to accommodate others whose personal behaviour is considered abhorrent.

A great deal of prison life is spent 'doing nothing'. In the remand centre this may involve long periods of time locked in a cell with three or four others. In the youth custody centre, there is more freedom, but trainees work around the farms and kitchens and chatter like the servants in the country house whose places they have usurped. Although in the first few days prisoners are almost afraid to talk about the world outside of the jail, in this episode there is a tendency to develop conversations about settings which are far away from prison. For example, one prisoner explains,

> 'We tend to talk about what has passed and we talk about the future. We don't tend to think about now. We talk about what we've done and we talk about what we aren't going to do in the future. And then we talk about what we are going to do in the future.'

Inevitably, conversation about past and future events comes to focus upon crime. There is a common-sense view that prisoners learn crime when placed in settings with other criminals. There is little empirical evidence to support this proposition and, by its very nature, this study cannot resolve this particular debate. However, the interviews with inmates of the remand and the youth custody centre help with an understanding of life inside prison and continuing criminality on discharge.

In the last episode, which covered the first days in prison, inmates talked little about their crimes or the events that led up to their remand to custody. In this episode, however, it is clear that established prisoners spend a deal of their time discussing each others' crimes. Much of the conversation is dramatised and exaggerated, a feature common to most prison talk. In their pursuit of companions, inmates will seek out others whom they find compatible. The evidence would suggest that, in consultation with trusted others, prisoners do learn simple criminal techniques from each other. This is not to say that they learn a new form of crime, rather that they discover a new skill within a familiar type of criminal behaviour. Thus, the burglar learns a new way to jemmy a window, the car thief the best place to steal a Ford Cortina. For example,

> 'It's amazing. You learn how to open windows with silly things.'

> 'You learn stupid little things like how to get into houses, the easy way to do it, like how to get into a car with a windscreen wiper, silly little things like that, which you'd never think of before. So being in here makes it easier.'

The acquisition of new delinquent skills may affect inmates' life on release from prison in two important respects. Firstly, the increased expertise will lead to more opportunities for the graduate and, as earlier chapters have shown, the coincidence of skill and opportunity is an important factor in the maintenance of a criminal career. Secondly, on release, the younger offender will have the confidence of knowing that many others pursue his lifestyle.

The sixteen year old house-breaker placed in a remand centre may be skilled and assured about continuing delinquency at the time of his arrest. On leaving the remand centre, this first-hand knowledge will be supplemented by the memories of other burglaries by fellow inmates. In short, the offender will have a mental picture of many other break-ins.

Indeed, amongst remandees and youth custody centre residents interviewed for this study, there was a feeling that placement in a penal institution contributed towards taking greater delinquent risks on release. However, the evidence does not suggest that prisoners stray easily from one crime to another. Indeed, all of the respondents had a clear idea about particular types of crime in which they would participate and a greater knowledge of sentencing procedure, which comes with a spell of prison custody, reinforces their 'conservatism'.

> 'I'm in here (the youth custody centre) for breaking into houses. And there's a lot of people like me, so I'm not alone first off. And I've had a chance to think about what went wrong last time and I've heard what went wrong for everybody else and I'm not going to make the same mistakes next time. It will probably end up the same with me in here, but I've got some ideas at least.'

Thus, there is little data to suggest that prisons are going to be very successful in reforming the recalcitrant young. By the time young offenders have reached a remand or youth custody centre they are set in their criminal ways and a violent shift in offending behaviour is unlikely to be effected by placement in an institution. This is just as well, as during his journey through the various custodial institutions, the property offender comes into contact with other, more serious, criminals. How do they bear upon the moral development and criminal identity of adolescent inmates?

In an institutional world made lean of outside stimulation, prisoners are attracted to the discussion of the emotive crimes of other inmates. As millions paw over misdemeanours embroidered upon in the *News of the World*, so inmates discuss the more uncommon crimes of their peers. However, unlike his compatriot about to enjoy Sunday lunch in the outside world, the incarcerated young offender can supplement his *hors-d'oeuvre* by meeting and talking with the key participant in the crime, such as the murderer or the rapist. The prisoner has the rather doubtful advantage of learning the assailant's perspective on the offence.

Such discussions appear to evoke sympathy between prisoners, although the acceptance of grave crimes is hidden beneath a thin veil of derision.

Crimes which are probably beyond the imagination of most property offenders and, for the most part, abhorrent, became validated in group discussion. Thus, the moral development of young delinquents accommodates the perpetrators of serious crimes although it in no way encourages participation. Often, however, the validation of offences such as murder is based upon the murderer's view of the crime. The discussion seldom focuses upon or empathises with the victim, thus reinforcing rules of behaviour identified in previous chapters.

During the first fieldwork visit in the remand centre, a great deal of discussion amongst inmates revolved around a well reported murder by a resident, of an Asian boy in a nearby town. Indeed, one of the group interviews was dominated by the subject and a consensus was reached by the participants that the assailant, with whom they had each shared a cell, should not be blamed for the murder. There was no suggestion that the respondents would act in a similar manner if faced with a similar situation, but the discussion, a tiny part of which is given below, does reveal something about the re-interpretation of serious crime.

> *Respondent One*: 'There's murder and there's murder and his was a good murder'
>
> *Respondent Two*: 'It ain't a good murder, all right so he's a Paki (an Asian boy), so then it could have easily been your old man or your old lady'
>
> *Respondent Three*: 'He said he admires thingy for murdering a Paki, right, well he wouldn't admire somebody for killing normal, he said he admired him for killing that one. Right? So that, in my view that's OK.'

Looking out; perceptions of the future

The preceding pages have described the harsh formal system imposed upon prisoners by the institution and the ability of inmates to create and maintain an informal system, to dramatise events and so compensate for the mundane existence, and to sympathise with other prisoners often at the expense of victims. Although this may mean that remand prisoners are well placed to move on within the prison system it also means that the youth custody centre residents are ill-prepared for the liberty to which they look forward. As a prison officer at the youth custody centre reports, the institutional environment is very unrealistic if it is intended to groom residents for future life.

'There are not many dairies in H_____ or B_____. There are fewer cabbage patches in A_____. So I think their environment is very unreal to them. There are times when the building is reversed, the building should be here for them, but they are sometimes here for the building, to keep its fabric going. I think it's wrong, but, there again, don't you tell anybody that.'

As has been found, much of the talk in the dairy and on the cabbage patch is of past and future crime. In considering the future, prisoners were found to be very realistic, especially those in the remand centre, many of whom faced a further period of detention in other prison department establishments. Almost all remandees were very clear about what to expect when their case was resolved as contact with other prisoners and previous periods of detention had furnished them with a good knowledge of length of sentence and of possible placements. For example, a burglar explains,

Burglar 'I'm up in Crown (Court) in about another two weeks'

Researcher 'And what do you expect to happen after that?'

Burglar 'I'll get about three years. Three years YC (Youth Custody). But I'll only do about 20 months. I'll almost certainly be going to (youth custody centre), should be OK.'

The period of remand also gives the prisoner ample time to prepare for the coming experience and most, who faced youth custody sentences, were able to play down the experience. Thus, the remandee who gave the preceding quotation was also able to remark,

'When I get there I'll not be worried. Well me mates will be there, and I've been to (the Local Prison) so I know what it's all about. It's just like this (the remand centre), but it's more scruffy and there's less room and it stinks.'

The youth custody centre inmates were able to look towards liberty in the near future. Few, when questioned thoroughly, gave any indication that they intended to stay within the formal, publicly stated rules on release. Indeed, in group discussions with the researcher those who claimed as much were derided.

Young prisoners are pragmatic in accepting future placement in prison and/or a return to criminal activity on release. Moreover, they appear to be unconcerned about their criminality. Life is treated as a waiting game, where some semblance of a 'normal' existence is created out of limited resources.

Once in the community, youth custody graduates return to a precarious criminal existence until re-capture leads to the relative certainty of prison. Whilst at liberty, inmates hope to avoid detection but view return to prison as extremely probable. The following quotation is a depressing reference to the continuing career ahead of those who are well experienced in the vagaries of custodial life. It also illustrates the confusion this young person feels when trying to describe the future.

> 'I'll go back out, try and get a job..... but I tried to get a job last time and look what happened. You know? I'll just have to find out what position I'm in. I hope I'll not be back inside again, but since I've been out this time, like, the robbery wasn't meant to be a robbery. Like before it was violence, robberies but burglary as well. Since I've been out we had four or five fights but that's about it. And all of them had good reasons, know what I mean? No gang fights, just one-to-one fights. That's about it. The only thing I can get into trouble for.'

Rules of behaviour

This chapter has focused upon the younger offender who is established in prison life. The inmate's presentation of self, the sanctions used to maintain the informal system, the relationship between different types of prisoner and perceptions of the future and discharge have been highlighted. What does this new evidence tell us about young property offenders' rules of behaviour when they are established in prison?

Societal rules

Once again, the societal rules operating in this episode are unchanged. However, the offender's relationship to these rules is different for, well established in prison, he will continually break a number of the prison laws, thus transgressing those societal rules which do apply in the institution. As release beckons he will be thinking about how he might break these societal rules concerning, for example burglary, which cannot apply in prison. Finally, as the prison officer comes to know the offender he is very likely to abandon reminders that offending is wrong and unjust as these are rules well known to the prisoner.

Societal rules

1. Do not offend
2. Do not steal

3. Do not injure
4. Do not break into houses
5. Do not steal from cars
6. Do not take and drive away cars
7. Do not kill somebody when you steal a car
8. Do not break into a house when somebody is in the house
9. Feel guilty for the things you have done wrong
10. Feel that offending is unjust.

Formal rules

The formal rules operating in this episode also differ little from those working in the preceding chapter dealing with the first few days in prison. Moreover, the rules still govern the life of the young person. The remand centre prisoners still have to get up and slop out at seven in the morning, the youth custody boys are still required to work in the kitchens or in the fields and all of the inmates will be locked in their cells or dormitories at night, some for a substantial proportion of the day. These formal rules will dog the young people under scrutiny in every penal institution they enter.

However, in this part of the criminal career there is much greater flexibility in the enforcement of formal rules. In a good institution it will be expected that the prison officer will be given some autonomy to decide when to enforce a rule and that certain misdemeanours will be overlooked. Indeed, the prison officer will be expected to support the inmate and help him with his personal problems. Thus, the formal rules in this episode also reflect the flexible and warmer side of the institution.

Formal rules

1. Failure to keep prison rules will result in sanctions
2. Prisoners who are found guilty of serious or repeated misconduct will be placed in solitary confinement
3. Prisoners will clean their cells daily
4. Remand prisoners will not throw urine/faeces out of the window
5. Prisoners will not accept cigarettes/matches from prison officers
6. Prisoners will not steal from one another
7. Prison officers may be lenient towards prisoners breaking rules in particular circumstances
8. Prison officers will enjoy some autonomy in enforcing prison rules
9. Prison officers will be supportive of prisoners
10. Prison officers will help prisoners with their personal problems

Belief and interaction rules

Whilst the prisoners' descriptions of the first few days in prison excludes the outside world and are devoted to the institutional regime, in the episode just described the talk is of the life beyond the prison walls and the daily routine is, wherever possible, ignored. Moreover, many of the belief rules operating in previous episodes, when the young person was free, recur in this chapter. The inmates are competitive and their individuality is emphasised.

There is clearly a gap between the belief and interaction rules operating in this episode. For example, as a previous quotation from a prison officer revealed, the belief rules will allow homosexual behaviour in particular contexts and sanction temporary adaptations necessary when heterosexual relationships are practically absent. However, in interaction, prisoners never talk about homosexuality; on the contrary, they emphasise their heterosexual prowess, and they make exaggerated displays of affection during girlfriends' visits. The presentation of self is very different from the actual behaviour.

The interaction rules of behaviour identified below are clearly functional to those who spend relatively long periods in closed conditions and are used by those anxious to put a brave face on a poor situation. Many belief rules of behaviour fit uneasily with institutional life. For example, competitive behaviour in surroundings which require high levels of co-operation could be a problem. However, with time the prisoner learns to let unmanageable emotions escape into the descriptions of fights used as sanctions against those who transgress the informal system. These events hold some significance for the inmates but, despite the violent depiction, little harm ever comes to the participants. Thus, interaction rules about sanctions, taking part in disputes no matter how trivial, standing one's ground and channelling unwanted emotions into highly embroidered descriptions of fight sequences have been identified.

There are further interaction rules about accommodating all types of criminal, including those remanded or sentenced for grave crimes such as murder or rape. However, it is noteworthy that not all of these interaction rules are yet fully developed. However, in interaction with each other and when presenting to the outside world, the prisoners profess to victimize inmates placed in custody for sex-crimes, a pattern common in adult prisons, but rare in remand and youth custody centres. Indeed, in the remand centre, vulnerable, older prisoners are placed with younger delinquents for their own protection and sympathy between offenders of all kinds has been discovered. A prison officer reinforced this observation when he said, 'They'll be telling you that the rapists and child molesters and granny bashers have got to watch out and in (a local prison) they do have to look out. But here they all live together, little kids learning the ropes, finding out what a rapist is!'

Belief rules

1. Emphasise your independence
2. Homosexual behaviour is acceptable in certain circumstances
3. Stand up for yourself in a conflict
4. Protect the name of your home community
5. Be competitive
6. Learn simple criminal techniques
7. Learn about the formal system (the juvenile justice system)
8. Accept that the future will involve further custodial experiences
9. Accept that you will offend again given the opportunity
10. Make the most of what you have got on release

Interaction rules

1. Maximise co-operation
2. Minimise conflict
3. Emphasise your heterosexual prowess
4. Make the most of girlfriends' visits
5. Make exaggerated displays of affection during girlfriends' visits
6. Fights will be arranged
7. Taking part is the most important aspect of a fight
8. While 'doing nothing' talk about the past or the future
9. Say that you will attack prisoners convicted or charged with sexual attacks against women
10. Talk to murderers and rapists about their crimes

Conclusions

In the episode studied in this chapter, whenever possible, the formal rules are subsumed into the informal system developed and maintained by inmates. The informal rules allow for an exaggerated presentation of self which is confusing to the uninitiated in the sense that the inmate appears to be in control of events and relatively unruffled by living conditions which are pretty dreadful. Those rules which guide interaction continue to be incongruous with the belief rules but this incongruity is functional in the sense that it contributes to the inflated identity of the young person and further ameliorates the impact of the formal system upon his life.

Finally, there are rules about preparing for the future and sustaining a criminal career. It has been seen that inmates acquire a few extra techniques within their particular area of delinquency each time they are placed in custody. This does not propel prisoners to a continuing life of crime, but most of those interviewed were clear that further offences, court appearances and prison sentences would follow in the future. There is little in the remand and the youth custody centre to divert residents away from their chosen life route and, in the absence of such prompts, the subjects of this study rationalise a continuing criminal identity and career.

Let us now bring all of the evidence put forward in the study in a re-examination of the hypotheses outlined in the opening chapter.

Summary Points

1. Prison life is presented by inmates in such a way that the tedium and less savoury aspects are hidden. This re-negotiation gives more dimensions to an otherwise limited existence.

2. Sanctions are used to maintain the informal social system. Physical violence or threat of physical violence form the principal sanctions.

3. Fights between inmates are orderly and planned. For the most part they are swift and they seldom require the intervention of the prison officer. Pugilists, adversaries in combat, have a respect for each other when the episode is complete.

4. Inmates dramatise fights and they can appear to be very violent. Thus, emotions which have little place in an environment that depends upon co-operation are channelled into aggressive descriptions.

5. The prisoners' tasks do not require much concentration and inmates spend a good deal of time musing over the activities of their peers. There is, however, little evidence that criminals learn new crimes, but they may acquire new techniques within an existing field of knowledge which offer more opportunities for delinquency.

6. It is suggested that meeting serious and violent offenders alters the moral perspectives of the burglar as he learns the assailant's view of his crime. There is little concern for victims.

7. Prison is an unrealistic environment in which to prepare a criminal for a crime-free life. Inmates expect to re-offend on achieving liberty and they sketch out future scenarios which suggest a continuing criminal career.

8. The ten most prominent societal, formal, belief and interaction rules operating in this period have been listed and discussed.

a) The societal rules remain the same in this episode but the inmate's relationship to them is different; he regularly breaks prison rules and expects to break state laws on release.

b) In this episode, there is much greater flexibility in the enforcement of formal rules; in a good institution, prison officers exercise considerable discretion.

c) The belief rules operating in this episode are very much concerned with life after prison. The inmate stresses his competitiveness and individuality, he accepts that release will lead to further delinquency. The inmate allows homosexuality as a component part of institutional life and, therefore, a criminal career.

d) The interaction rules are concerned with putting a brave face on a poor situation; continued imprisonment. Interaction rules accommodate the serious offender and they mask homosexual liaisons.

10. Conclusions

The preceding pages offered an explanation for persistent offending which focused upon the young offenders' perspective of events. This has been achieved by examining the social identity of the young persistent property offender. Erikson (1956) has described the process whereby adolescents between the ages of 16 and 24 choose particular aspects of an identity but suppress others. In this study, this process is examined through a method based on the perspectives of Harré and Secord (1972). This approach separates the criminal career into episodes and identifies the component rules of behaviour operating in each episode. A 'career' has been defined for the purposes of this study as a course through life in which the individual's choice between options holds the key to his or her progress. An 'episode' has been taken to mean a variable period of time surrounding a particular phase of the delinquent career. Rules provide a framework for social behaviour, they have an undoubted influence upon the final form of individual conduct, but they are continuously adapted and changed by the participants during each social episode.

Using this method, four episodes in the young person's criminal career have been explored. In the first, the early days in the criminal career came under scrutiny, during which the young offender first breaks into strangers' houses or cars. This episode was followed by an examination of life on the margins of prison when another arrest will almost certainly see the young person remanded to custody or, if convicted, sentenced to youth custody. Indeed, in the next episode, the young offender was seen coping with his first days in a remand or youth custody centre. Finally, the preceding chapter explored the life of a young offender established in prison and reconciled to a continuing criminal career.

At the beginning of this study, in order to aid a systematic analysis of the developing criminal identity of the young men, five theoretical propositions were advanced. Initially, it was suggested that delinquents choose a criminal identity based upon a series of decisions which appear rational to them. Secondly, it was proposed that, in exercising his choice, the young offender uses guidelines shared by those who have an empathy with his lifestyle. Thirdly, it was suggested that evidence based upon the young offender's perspective would show that the juvenile justice system contributed to the criminal identity. Fourthly, the idea that the persistent delinquent presents a criminal identity even when that identity is no longer congruous with his current behaviour was offered. Finally, it was proposed that the delinquent identity changes and develops during each of the four episodes under scrutiny.

In this final chapter, these theoretical propositions will be re-considered in the light of other writers' work and the evidence from the remand and the youth custody centre just discussed. However, the interactionist perspective which guided the research is but one of a number of attempts to explain crime and delinquency amongst the young. Thus, in the final pages, the relationship between the findings of this study and other explanations is considered.

Let us begin by exploring the propositions outlined in Chapter One. Does the persistent delinquent looked at in this study choose an identity based upon a series of decisions which appear rational to him and does this identity develop throughout the criminal career?

Choice and the developing criminal identity

It has been seen from other studies of adolescent development that it is not uncommon for people to choose careers which end badly. Many examples are available, but particularly vivid is Cressey's (1932) study of Taxi-dancers, women initially hired as dance partners for men, who later graduate to prostitution. Despite massive social pressures to the contrary, many groups in our society persist with non-conformist careers.

A number of writers have focused upon the decisions that lead individuals to choose one career rather than another. Becker and Strauss (1956) are interested in the first step in commissioning a new career, the first delinquency, the initial interest of the musician in jazz, the drug user's original smoke of marijuana. The key decision for the young people scrutinized in this study, however, has not been their initial delinquency; many youngsters break the law as part of ordinary adolescent experimentation. Rather, the important decisions have been to persist with relatively serious crimes in the face of successive police cautions and prosecutions in court. Why do young people continue to break into houses in the face of family despair, removal from home, school and friends and other discouraging features of their life, all of which are as painful as a court appearance?

It is clear from the evidence presented in this study that the 'choice' of a criminal career involves the acceptance of some features of an identity but the rejection of others. It is clear that the young offender drifts into situations which are likely to lead to delinquency but that the decision to offend is a combination of the opportunity, skill and bravado required to see the event through. Furthermore, by choosing to continue with his criminal lifestyle, the young offender closes a number of doors which might otherwise have led to conformity and extended liberty, particularly such important options as those which hold out the promise of education, employment and security.

It is also apparent from the preceding pages that the public and private perceptions of the persistent delinquent are very different and that the criminal identity may not always be as it seems to the uninitiated. Criminal behaviour, even among the delinquent group of young people studied here, is a very rare event; most of the time they are law abiding. For the majority, participation in relatively serious crime such as car theft would take place on fewer than half a dozen days per year and be viewed as no more than a 'moral holiday' (Box 1981). In contrast to the sporadic nature of offending within a criminal career, the intervention of statutory agencies in the life of the young offender can be continuous with successive supervision, care and probation orders, not to speak of sentences to detention and youth custody centres. The criminal behaviour is occasional but the public response to it is continuous and the criminal identity is reinforced by repeated reminders from those in authority as to the consequences.

Although the first public response to delinquency is sudden and can appear to the young offender who has evaded detection many times as a random response, the criminal identity develops through a number of subtle changes. It has been seen that, in the initial episodes, the offender chooses to break the law because it is exciting and enjoyable and, while it reaps little material reward, it brings immediate gratification and status to small groups of delinquents. Although they freely choose to steal a car, the young people do not, at this stage, take into account the long-term consequences of their actions. They risk serious injury and charges if they crash the stolen car and, in any case, they are likely to incur the long term interest of statutory authorities.

As the career progresses, the offender becomes more calculating in his behaviour and weighs more carefully the benefits and risks of his actions. He carefully revises previous responses to his delinquency into a more coherent identity, thus the intermediate treatment officer's threat that he will never get a job holds no sway as gainful employment is not viewed as a positive attribute. Similarly, appeals to consider the victims of crime are likely to have little effect as the offender does not know for whom or about what to feel guilty. He is not interested in them because they are not interested in him.

As his peers become increasingly reluctant to continue with a delinquent lifestyle, as the courts impose sanctions which separate him from more law abiding friends and as he decides to secure greater financial reward for his endeavours, the young offender becomes more solitary in his delinquent behaviour. He becomes increasingly skilled and confident and begins to tap into other criminal networks which will help to launder the booty or alert him to further possibilities of crime. Increasingly, the young offender makes choices from limited options and, as he becomes well known to the police and courts, the career begins to take on a momentum of its own.

During the episodes in prison it has been possible to examine more closely the developing identity. The preceding pages have borne witness to inmates who appear bewildered, disorientated and lost during their first days in prison but increasingly gain confidence and adapt to institutional life with all its disadvantages. The pains of institutional life, the absence of privacy, separation from family and friends and enforced liaison with other criminals have to be coped with and success comes from endurance, acceptance and bearing incarceration with dignity.

The institution attempts to strip the inmate of his identity but he fights off anonymity by identifying with other prisoners. He adapts to his surroundings and pursues activities, such as trips to the library, education class and workshop which would be anathema in his previous existence. In these strange surroundings, he joins in and contributes to the informal social world of the prison which, together with its formal counterpart, help the institution to function. The most important aspect of these findings, as far as the criminal identity is concerned, is that the young offender finds he is able to cope with the most severe response of society to his delinquent lifestyle and finds himself playing a positive part in the daily life of a large institution.

Let us briefly summarise these findings regarding choice and development of a criminal identity. Initially, although persistent property offending is an unusual response, many people commit themselves to careers that end badly; that is to say they do not result in an outcome most parents would wish for their own children. The first decision to act in a delinquent fashion is undoubtedly important but choice of a continuing criminal career when all around are abandoning the behaviour has also been stressed. The choice has negative and positive components as the young people actively pursue some options and, as a consequence, find other routes closed. The decisions made towards a career choice appear rational to the offender but the rationale differs between the episodes of the criminal career; at first excitement, later financial reward, later still the maintenance of a criminal identity. At each stage, the young offender copes with and incorporates into his identity the disposals made by the court. Particularly important in this process is the response of others who share his chosen lifestyle. Indeed, let us now explore the relationship which the persistent young property offender shares with family and friends as the question is asked, does the offender use shared guidelines in exercising his choice of identity?

Shared guidelines and the choice of identity

The evidence from social psychological studies reviewed in Chapter Four explains the dynamics of small groups of adolescents contravening the dominant moral order, occasionally indulging in crime. To an extent, these findings fit well with sub-cultural explanations of delinquency which view crime as acceptable within particular peer groups and Sutherland and Cressey's (1970) theory of differential association in which young people choose to obey some state laws but reject others. However, whilst these explanations fit well for the petty delinquency that characterizes the majority of adolescent crime, it was unclear whether they could be applied to more serious crime.

The new evidence gathered for this study has revealed changing patterns of association for those who choose a criminal identity. As has been stated, early criminal expeditions are joint ventures of four or five young people, responding to an absence of anything to 'do'. Once they are caught, this experimentation assumes new meaning. The offender finds that his family are outraged, as one inmate recalled, 'You expect your mum and dad to be sorry for you if you are in a car crash, but when you have stolen the car they don't seem all that worried.' Furthermore, although there are many who will 'try out' a burglary, there are few who will continue in the face of initial warnings, for example cautions from the police. The offender discussed in this study finds that his friends disengage from the behaviour, but remain interested in his identity. However, in order to maintain this status, the persistent delinquent must seek out others who share a similar experience, can empathise with his situation and offer some guidance on what are the likely outcomes.

The continued interest of the statutory agencies, for example social services, probation and the prison service also make liaisons with the home community difficult to maintain. Unintentionally, they tend to restrict the interactions of the offender to those with similar lifestyles. Moreover, with increasing confidence and experience, the persistent delinquent assumes the argot and style of an older, hardened offender. As he talks of the 'big job' and wishes for the 'end of my time (sentence)', the young offender discussed in this study becomes increasingly out of tune with his home community although he will treat previous peer groups and family as an interested audience to whom he can recount his exploits. He is well equipped, however, to tap into the margins of other criminal networks, for example the scrap yards which buy and sell stolen cars or those anxious for car radios.

However, whilst the interventions of the state sever some of the young offender's relationships, it also introduces others into his life. Most of these new liaisons are with criminals. However, it would be wrong to assume that all ground is common to fellow offenders. For example, it has been shown in Chapter Five that prisoners in the remand and youth custody centres have enjoyed widely divergent cultural experiences and possess varying knowledge of crime and the juvenile justice system. Moreover, the persistent delinquent is identified in Chapter Seven as a solitary creature. Thus, the first few days in prison are characterized not by instant co-operation and mateyness but by hesitant negotiation.

Indeed, in Chapter Eight the analysis of the group dynamics of the prisoners in the remand centre revealed an absence of strong leaders and highlighted fluid hierarchies which change in response to particular situations. The overall evidence assembled in this study suggests that shared guidelines are important in the developing criminal identity but that patterns of interaction are subtle and changing. Thus, whilst there is support for the idea that groups of offenders learn from each other, cold water can be poured on the contamination theory that one bad apple spoils the barrel.

A major influence upon the young offender's patterns of interaction is clearly the intervention of the statutory authorities. Let us now explore whether, as proposed at the beginning, the juvenile justice system contributes to the criminal identity and also examine the congruity of identity and behaviour.

The juvenile justice system, the criminal identity and criminal behaviour

Initially, it should be clear from the evidence presented in this study that the juvenile justice system is a complex series of hurdles and processes with a variety of goals and functions including, for example, punishment, reform and the welfare of the offender. It is also apparent from the preceding pages that there is an important distinction between the legal system and the offender's experience of it. This research has revealed aspects of both and it is clear that the prison officer can have as great an impact upon the lives of the persistent delinquent as other prisoners.

In any discussion of the impact of the juvenile justice system upon the young offender, it is necessary to remember that entry to the system is carefully controlled and, usually, only the very persistent find an easy entrance. As has been seen, the young people discussed in this study have been undeterred by police cautions or by a wide variety of community-based interventions. The majority of offenders known to statutory bodies have unsatisfactory family backgrounds and have undergone a range of preparatory experience including residential care. However, there is no strict tariff adhered to by the courts when disposing of the offender's crime and, while it is possible to identify common episodes in the criminal career, there are a number of variations in the young people's experience of the juvenile justice system.

How do these experiences shape the criminal identity? It has been seen that there is a considerable literature which purports to show how the wider society can reinforce the deviant identity through stigma, social labels and institutionalisation. However, previous studies have been reticent to explore the mechanics of this process and none has related it directly to the lives of persistent young property offenders. In the later chapters of this study, many of these gaps have been filled with the exploration of the offender's separation from family and home community, the disqualification from school and the steady evaporation of law-abiding friends. However, once again, the evidence suggests that the impact of the wider society and the juvenile justice system is a complicated process which is bound up with the various informal and formal rules which act as a guide to behaviour.

Other writers have explored in some depth the relationship between the informal and formal components of social life. Merton (1938,1957) has offered the informal adaptations of rebellion, manipulation and conformity amongst those who cannot meet the formal expectations of society. Willis (1977) has shown how informal acting out in the classroom is functional in that it prepares for the formal society's need for manual labour. Millham, Bullock and Cherrett (1975) have shown how the daily routine of an institution reflects the balance between the formal and informal goals of its members. The study in hand has tackled this complex relationship in a variety of situations.

The theoretical approach described in Chapter Two identified various types of rule which guide criminal behaviour, but which also strongly influence the criminal identity. Firstly, there are *societal rules*, which change little over time and which remain constant between different settings. For example, it is wrong to steal in the community, it is also wrong to steal in prison. The societal rules, however, are adapted in different formal contexts, for example, by the police, the courts and in prison, thus creating a second tier of *formal rules*. Thirdly, there are the informal rules created and used by the young people under scrutiny to guide their interaction in different contexts; these are referred to as *interaction rules*. Finally, a fourth tier of *belief rules* are adopted by the offenders. The preceding pages have charted the changing relationship between these four types of rules acting as a guide to criminal behaviour; this relationship is best summarised in the following diagram:

Figure 12.1 The relationship between four rules of behaviour in four episodes of the criminal career.

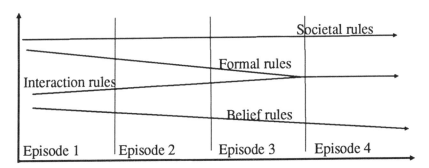

The graph shows how societal rules are constant throughout each of the four episodes under examination and that there is growing incongruity between formal and societal rules, because the rules of the context bend to accommodate the 'known' facts about the offender. However, as the career develops, the interaction rules are in increasing harmony with the societal and formal rules because the young offender has to get by in a series of increasingly controlled situations. However, while interaction and belief rules are congruous at the beginning of episode one, they are very incongruous by the end of episode four; one of the enduring characteristics of reformatory efforts is a concentration on the relationship between societal, formal and interaction rules at the expense of belief rules. Thus, although the offender behaves in prison, he remains unreformed. This theoretical model is best illustrated with examples from each of the episodes studied.

The first episode concerned the first excursions into relatively serious crime, such as car theft. During this time, the delinquency is both viewed and described by the offender as petty, unplanned, enjoyable and exciting. Moreover, the rules which allow the initiation of this behaviour are very different from those which ensure its persistence, for at this stage the delinquent is very unsure about continued law-breaking. However, this unfettered attitude, which sees harmony between interaction and belief rules, leads to disharmony with the formal and societal rules, many of which the offender breaks and, with his general licence to enjoy, he risks contravening many more. Moreover, being caught invokes a new set of formal rules which are relevant to the police caution and court disposal, for example complying with the demands of an intermediate treatment order.

In the second episode to be scrutinized, the offender is on the margins of prison and he finds fewer peers anxious to participate in his criminal endeavours. There is a strain in his relationships and he has to find new ways of describing his delinquency and his experience of statutory authorities. This leads to growing incongruity between interaction and belief rules. On the other hand, as he becomes more skilled in his offending, he reduces the risk of accidental law breaking and there is greater congruence between formal and interaction rules.

In the third episode, the offender is to be found enduring his first days in prison. As he feels insecure and frightened, the young prisoner follows the formal publicly stated rules of the institution. In the final episode, the interaction rules are increasingly incongruous with the belief rules but this incongruity is functional in the sense that it maintains the identity of the prisoner and ameliorates the impact of the formal system upon his life. For example, the belief rules may allow homosexuality, which is contrary to the societal rules, tolerated by the formal rules of the institution and placed under a veil by the interaction rules which stress heterosexual prowess.

In summary, this evidence shows that as the interaction and formal rules become congruous, the juvenile justice system reinforces the criminal identity. The offender takes in his stride and incorporates into his identity the state response to his delinquency. However, the interaction rules are now very different from the belief rules suggesting that the behaviour is no longer synchronous with the identity.

It is noteworthy that as the criminal career develops, there is growing divergence between the formal and societal rules as those who deal with the young offender adapt to the statutory obligations. Indeed, it would have been most interesting to increase the scope of the career under scrutiny and to separate it into more episodes in a very intensive way, for example, looking at the different rules operating in the police station and in the court. A continuing scrutiny of the rules operating later in the career when, as Rutherford (1986) suggests, the offender grows out of crime would also merit further research.

Conclusions and the relevance of the study to other research

It has been shown that using an interactionist approach with a systematic approach to the interpretation of data the theoretical propositions previously forwarded hold true. Delinquency is a choice and the different decisions that lead to that choice at different stages in the career are all seen by the offender as rational. The role of others sympathetic to the identity is key and the change in identity during the career is self-evident. Using a method to reveal rules of behaviour has led to an examination of the relationship between the formal and informal aspects of social life in a new way and has revealed some of the subtle contributions of the juvenile justice system to the criminal career as well as disclosing the increasing disparity between identity and behaviour.

However, whilst there has never been a claim to provide the last word on or to attempt causal explanations of delinquency, it must be emphasised that the approach applied in this study is only one of many. Rutter and Giller (1983) list twelve explanations of juvenile delinquency, a number of which have been reviewed in this volume. Delinquency can be viewed as a consequence of: anomie; sub-cultural processes; differential association; the lack of social controls; learned responses; family processes; primitive urges; biological processes; the situations in which the young offender finds him or herself; the limited options available to the offender; labelling; and as a reaction to the rituals of society. What does the evidence offered in this study say about these perspectives? Apart from addressing apparently contradictory aspects of the criminal career, for example continuing delinquency despite a lack of material rewards and in the face of the pains of imprisonment; apart from applying a new type of method to the subject area; apart from linking the informal and formal components of the delinquent's world in a new way and exposing the difference between the public and private perception of juvenile crime; what else does the study say which is new?

By tackling delinquency as a career and by looking at this career from the perspective of the offender, the study helps to link some of the causal chains and processes outlined by Rutter and Giller (1983). The research has not dealt with the biological processes of delinquency or viewed it as a manifestation of primitive urges. However, theories of differential association and sub-culture have been successfully adapted in this study to show how the young offender makes sense of and chooses between the variety of messages coming from his home community about his delinquency. The previous pages have charted the relationship between the formal and informal social worlds of the young offender giving insight into the way he perceives the response of the wider society to his delinquency thus giving new perspectives on theories of anomie, labelling and reaction to rituals.

Moreover, this study explains those processes which lead groups of people to make apparently lunatic choices and to act in seemingly self-destructive ways. It has been seen that the offender is well aware of many of the theoretical observations listed by Rutter and Giller; he knows that the police are particularly interested in his delinquent activity and he knows that the courts will deal with his future offences differently than it would those of a first offender. But the young people scrutinised in this study rationalise these social handicaps and incorporate these messages into social identity in such a way that continued delinquency is assured.

Furthermore, the explanations detailed in the previous pages are relevant to people who do not display unique psychological traits but, like the majority of young offenders, have apparently intractable conduct disorders. The study has explained how a delinquent identity is built up and maintained. It has proffered a series of answers to questions about the persistence in the behaviour of a delinquent who is not biologically handicapped. It can be seen from the preceding pages how a small group of persistent property offenders incorporate features of their social experience into a desired, if unsatisfactory, outcome.

This study is unlikely to alter the feelings of horror or disbelief felt by those unlucky enough to return from a pleasant evening to find their homes ransacked or for those victims of car theft hopefully surveying the car park for their missing vehicle. However, the research gives practitioners, policy makers and others concerned with young offenders new insights into delinquency. In addition, the study suggests to those anxious to offer an interactionist perspective a method of systematically analysing the interpretations people make about their lifestyle.

Bibliography

ARGYLE, M. (1967), *Psychology and Social Problems*, London: Social Science Paperbacks.

ARGYLE, M. (1969), *Social Interaction*, London: Social Science Paperbacks.

ARGYLE, M. (1978), 'Discussion chapter: an appraisal of the new approach to the study of social behaviour' in Brenner M., Marsh P. and Brenner M. (eds.), *The Social Contexts of Method*. London: Croom-Helm.

ATHELSTAN, *Judicia Civitatis Lundaniae sub rege Aethalstano edita*, 10th Century.

++++

BALES, R.F. (1950), *Interaction Process Analysis; a Method for the Study of Small Groups*. Cambridge, Mass: Addison-Wesley.

BALES, R.F. (1958), 'Task roles and social roles in problem solving groups' in MacCoby E.E., Newcomb T.M. and Hartley E.L. (eds.), *Readings in Social Psychology*, New York: Holt.

BALL, S.J. (1983), 'Case study research in education: some notes and problems' in Hammersley M. (ed.), *The Ethnography of Schooling, Methodological Issues*, Driffield: Nafferton.

BARTAK, L. and RUTTER, M. (1975), 'The measurement of staff-child interaction in three units for autistic children' in Tizard J., Sinclair I. and Clarke R.V.G. (eds.), *Varieties of Residential Experience*, London: Routledge & Kegan Paul,

BECKER, G.S. (1968), 'Crime and punishment: an economic approach', *Journal of Political Economy*, 76, 169-217.

BECKER, H.S. (1958), 'Problems of inference and proof in participant observation', *American Sociological Review*, 23, (Dec.), pp. 652-659.

BECKER, H.S. (1963), *Outsiders: Studies in the Sociology of Deviance*. New York: Free Press.

BECKER, H.S. and GEER, B. (1960), 'Participant observation: the analysis of qualitative field data' in Adams R.N. and Preiss J.J. (eds.), *Human Organisation Research, Field Relations and Techniques*, Illinois: Davsey Press.

BECKER, H.S. and STRAUSS, A.L. (1956), 'Careers, personality and adult socialization', *American Journal of Sociology*, LX11, Nov., 3, pp.253-263.

BEHAN, B. (1958), *Borstal Boy*, London: Hutchinson.

BELSON, W.A. and HOOD, R. (1967), *The Research Potential of Case Records of Approved - School Boys*, Survey Research Centre Report No. 6.

BERGER, P. and LUCKMAN, T. (1971), *The Social Construction of Reality*, Harmondsworth: Allen Lane.

BETTLEHEIM, B. (1960), *The Informed Heart, A Study of the Psychological Consequences of Living under Extreme Fear and Terror*, New York: Free Press.

BISHOP, N. (1960), 'Group work at Pollington Borstal', *Howard Journal*, 10, No. 3, 185.

BLACK, M. (1972), *The Labyrinth of Language*, Harmondsworth: Penguin.

BOTTOMS, A.E. and McCLINTOCK, F.H. (1973), *Criminals Coming of Age*, London: Heinemann.

BOX, S. (1981), *Deviance, Reality and Society*, Eastbourne: Holt, Rinehart and Winston.

BOYLE, J. (1977), *A Sense of Freedom*, London: Pan Books.

BRAKE, M. (1980), *The Sociology of Youth Culture and Youth Sub-Culture*, London: Routledge & Kegan Paul.

BREAKWELL, G. (1986), *Coping with Threatened Identities*, London: Methuen.

BROWN, R. (1965), *Social Psychology*, New York: Free Press.

BULLOCK, R., HAAK, M., HOSIE, K., MILLHAM, S. and MITCHELL, L. (1983), *Children Remanded to Care: a Study of Children Remanded to Care under Section 23 (1) of the 1969 Children and Young Persons Act*, unpublished Research Report; Dartington Social Research Unit.

BULMER, M. (1982), 'Ethical problems in social research; the case of participant observation' in *Social Research Ethics*, London: MacMillan.

++++

CAMPBELL, A. (1984), *The Girls in the Gang: A Report from New York City*, Oxford: Blackwell.

CARTER, L.F. (1954), 'Recording and evaluating the performance of individuals and members of small groups', *Personal Psychology*, 1954, VII, 477-484.

CERNKOVICH, S.A. and GIORDANO, P.C. (1979), 'A comparative analysis of male and female delinquency', *Sociological Quarterly*, 20, 131-45.

CLARKE, R.V.G. (1987), 'Rational choice theory and prison psychology', in McGurk B.J., Thornton, D.M. and Williams, M. *Applying Psychology to Imprisonment: Theory and Practice*, London: HMSO.

CLARKE, R.V.G. and CORNISH, D.B (1975), *Residential Treatment and Its Effects*, London: HMSO.

CLARKE, R.V.G. and MARTIN, D.N. (1971), *Absconding from Approved Schools*, Home Office Research Study No. 12, London: HMSO.

CLEMMER, D. (1958), *The Prison Community*, New York: Holt, Rhinehart and Winston.

CLINE, H. and WHEELER, S. (1968), 'The determinants of normative patterns in penal institutions' in Christie N. (ed.) (1968) *Scandanavian Studies in Criminology*, 2. London: Tavistock.

COHEN, A.K. (1955), *Delinquent Boys: The Culture of the Gang*, New York: Free Press.

COHEN, S. (1972), *Folk Devils and Moral Panics*, London: MacGibbon and Kee.

COHEN, S. and TAYLOR, L. (1977), *Prison Secrets*, London: Radical Alternatives to Prison.

COHEN, S. and TAYLOR, L. (1981), *Psychological Survival: The Experience of Long Term Imprisonment*, Harmondsworth: Penguin.

COLLETT P. (1974), 'The rules of conduct' in Collett, P. (ed.), *Social Rules and Social Behaviour*, Oxford: Blackwell.

CORRIGAN, P. (1979), *Schooling the Smash Street Kids*, London: MacMillan.

CRESSEY, P.G. (1932), *The Taxi-Dance Hall*, Chicago: University of Chicago Press.

++++

DENZIN, N.K. (1970), *Sociological Methods: A Sourcebook*, London: Butterworths.

DUNLOP, A.B. and McCABE, S. (1965), *Young Men in Detention Centres*, London: Routledge & Kegan Paul.

++++

ELKIND, D. (1979), *The Child and Society, Essays in Applied Child Development*, New York: OUP.

EMERY, F.E. (1970), *Freedom and Justice Within Walls: The Bristol Prison Experiment*, London: Tavistock.

ERIKSON, E.H. (1956), 'The problem of ego-identity', *American Journal of Psychoanalytic Association*, 4, 56-121.

ERIKSON, K.T. (1964), 'Notes on the sociology of deviance' in Becker H.S. *The Other Side: Perspectives on Deviance*, New York: Free Press.

ERICKSON, K.T. (1966), *Wayward Puritans*, London: John Wiley.

ETZIONI, A. (1961), *A Comparative Analysis of Complex Organisations*, Chicago: Free Press.

++++

FILSTEAD, W.J. (ed) (1970), *Qualitative Methodology: First Hand Involvement with the Social World*, Chicago: Markham.

FITZGERALD, M. and SIM, J. (1979), *British Prisons*, Oxford: Blackwell.

FOUCAULT, M. (1977), *Discipline and Punish: The Birth of the Prison*, Harmondsworth: Allen Lane.

++++

GARFINKEL, H. (1967), *Studies in Ethnomethodology*, Englewood-Cliffs: Prentice-Hall.

GIALLOMBARDO, R. (1966), *Society of Women: A study of a Women's Prison*, New York: John Wiley.

GIDDENS, A. (1976), *New Rules of Sociological Method*, London: Hutchinson.

GLADSTONE REPORT (1895), *Report from the Departmental Committee on Prisons*, Cmnd. 7702.

GLASER, B.G., and STRAUSS, A.L. (1967), *The Discovery of Grounded Theory*, Chicago: Aldine.

GLASER, D. (1964), *The Effectiveness of a Prison and Parole System*, Indianapolis: Bobbs - Merrill.

GOFFMAN, E. (1959), *The Presentation of Self in Everyday Life*, London: Allen Lane.

GOFFMAN, E. (1961), *Asylums*, Harmondsworth: Penguin.

GOFFMAN, E. (1963), *Stigma: Notes on the Management of Spoiled Identity*, Englewood-Cliffs: Prentice-Hall.

GOFFMAN, E. (1981), *Forms of Talk*, Oxford: Blackwell.

GOLD, M. (1966), 'Undetected Delinquent Activity', *Journal of Research into Crime and Delinquency*, 3, pp.27-46.

GULLIVER, P.H. (1963), *Social Control in an African Society*, London:

GUMB, R. (1972), *Rule Governed Linguistic Behaviour*, The Hague: Mouton.

GURIN, P. and TOWNSEND, A. (1986), 'Properties of Gender Identity and the Implication for Gender Consciousness', *British Journal of Social Psychology*, 25, 139-148.

++++

HALL, S. and JEFFERSON, T. (1976), *Resistance through Rituals*, London: Hutchinson.

HAMMERSLEY, M. and ATKINSON, P. (1983), *Ethnography: Principles in Practice*, London: Tavistock.

HARGREAVES, D. (1967), *Social Relations in a Secondary School*, London: Routledge & Kegan Paul.

HARGREAVES, D.M., HESTER, S.K. and MELLOR, F.J. (1975), *Deviance in Classrooms*, London: Routledge & Kegan Paul.

HARRÉ, R. (1978), 'Accounts, actions and meanings. The practice of participatory psychology' in Brenner, M., Marsh P. and Brenner, M. (eds.), *The Social Contexts of Method*, London: Croom Helm.

HARRÉ, R. (1979), *Social Being*, Oxford: Blackwell.

HARRÉ, R. and SECORD, P.F. (1972), *The Explanation of Social Behaviour*: Oxford: Blackwell.

HARRÉ, R., CLARKE, D. and DE CARLO, N. (1985), *Motives and Mechanisms: An Introduction to the Psychology of Action*, London: Methuen.

HINDESS, B. (1973), *The Use of Official Statistics in Sociology: A Critique of Positivism and Ethnomethodology*, London: Macmillan.

HIRSCHI, T. (1969), *Causes of Delinquency*, Berkeley: University of California Press.

HOME OFFICE (1959), *Penal Practice in a Changing Society: Aspects of Future Development*, Cmnd. 645, London: HMSO.

HOME OFFICE (1974), *Young Adult Offenders: Report of the Advisory Council on the Penal System*, London: HMSO.

HOME OFFICE (1977), *Prisons and the Prisoner: The Work of the Prison Service in England and Wales*, London: HMSO.

HOME OFFICE (1981), *Criminal Statistics, England and Wales, 1980*, London: HMSO.

HOME OFFICE (1982), *Unrecorded Offences of Burglary and Theft in a Dwelling in England and Wales: Estimates from the General Household Survey*, Home Office Statistical Bulletin, 11/82.

HOME OFFICE (1983), *The British Crime Survey: First Report* by Hough, M. and Mayhew, P., London: HMSO.

HOME OFFICE (1984), *Criminal Statistics England and Wales, 1983*, London: HMSO.

HOME OFFICE (1984b), *Remands in Custody: the Government Reply to the First Report from the Home Affairs Committee, Session 1983-84 HC 252*, London: HMSO.

HOME OFFICE (1984c), *Tougher Regimes in Detention Centres: Report of an Evaluation by the Young Offender Psychology Unit*, London: HMSO.

HOME OFFICE (1985), *Criminal Statistics, England and Wales, 1984*, London: HMSO.

HOME OFFICE (1986), *Criminal Statistics, England and Wales, 1985*. London: HMSO.

HOOD, R. (1965), *Borstal Re-assessed*, London: Heinemann.

HOOD, R. and SPARKS, R. (1970), *Key Issues in Criminology*, London: Weidenfeld and Nicholson.

HUMPHRIES, S. (1981), *Hooligans or Rebels? An Oral History of Working Class Childhood and Youth 1889-1939*, Oxford: Blackwell.

++++

INHELDER, B. and PIAGET, J. (1958), *The Growth of Logical Thinking*, New York: Basic Books.

IREMONGER, T.L. (1962), *Disturbers of the Peace*, London: Johnson.

IRWIN, J. (1970), *The Felon*, Englewood Cliffs: Prentice-Hall

++++

JONES, H. (1973), 'Approved schools and attitude change', *British Journal of Criminology*, XIII, pp. 148-56.

++++

KING, R.D. and MORGAN, R. (1976), *A Taste of Prison: Custodial Conditions for Trial and Remand Prisoners*, London: Routledge & Kegan Paul.

KING, R.D. and ELLIOT, K.W. (1977), *Albany: Birth of a Prison - End of an Era*, London: Routledge & Kegan Paul.

KITSUSE, J. (1972), 'Deviance, deviant behaviour and deviants: some conceptual issues' in W.J. Filstead (ed.), *An Introduction to Deviance*, Chicago: Markham Books.

KOHLBERG, L. (1969), 'Stage and sequence. The cognitive development approach to socialization' in Goslin, D.A. (ed), *Handbook of Socialization Theory and Research*, Chicago: Rand McNally.

++++

LAMBERT, R. and MILLHAM, S. (1968), *The Hothouse Society: an Explanation of Boarding School Life through the Boys' and Girls' Own Writings*, London: Weidenfeld and Nicolson.

LAMBERT, R., BULLOCK, R. and MILLHAM, S. (1975), *The Chance of a Lifetime: A Study of Boarding Education*, London: Weidenfeld and Nicolson.

LAMBERT, R., MILLHAM, S. and BULLOCK R. (1970), *A Manual to the Sociology of the School*, London: Weidenfeld and Nicolson.

LAMBERT, R., MILLHAM, S. and BULLOCK R. (1973), 'The informal social system' in Brown, R.K. (ed.), *Knowledge, Education and Cultural Change, Papers in the Sociology of Education*, London: Tavistock.

LECKY, P. (1945), *Self-Consistency, a Theory of Personality*, New York: Island Press.

LEMERT, E. (1951), *Social Pathology*, New York: McGraw Hill.

LLEWELLIN, W.W. (1933), 'Lowdham Grange - a borstal experiment', *Howard Journal* 3, No.4. 36.

LOWSON, D. (1970), *City Lads in Borstal*, Liverpool: Liverpool University Press.

LUCKMAN, T. (ed) (1978), *Phenomenology and Sociology, Selected Readings*, Harmondsworth: Penguin.

++++

McCLINTOCK, F.H. and GIBSON, E. (1961), *Robbery in London*, London: Macmillan.

McVICAR, J. (1979), *McVicar: By Himself*, London: Arrow Books.

MANNHEIM, H. and WILKINS, L.T. (1955), *Prediction Methods in Relation to Borstal Training*, London: HMSO.

MARSH, P. (1978), *Aggro: The Illusion of Violence*, London: Dent.

MARSH, P. (1978b), 'Life and careers on the soccer terraces' in Ingham R., Hall S., Clarke J., Marsh P. and Donovan J., *Football Hooliganism: The Wider Context*, London: Inter-Action Imprint.

MARSH, P. and CAMPBELL, A. (1982), *Aggression and Violence*, Oxford: Blackwell.

MARSH, P., ROSSER, E. and HARRÉ, R. (1978), *The Rules of Disorder*, London: Routledge & Kegan Paul.

MATZA, D. (1962), 'Position and behaviour patterns of youth' in E. Faris (ed.), *Handbook of Modern Sociology*, New York: Rand McNally.

MATZA, D. (1964), *Delinquency and Drift*, New York: John Wiley.

MATZA, D. (1969), *Becoming Deviant*, Englewood Cliffs: Prentice-Hall.

MATZA, D. and SYKES, G. (1957), 'Techniques of neutralization', *American Sociological Review*, 22 Dec. pp. 664-70.

MATZA, D. and SKYES, G. (1961), 'Juvenile delinquency and sub-terranean values', *American Sociological Review*, 26, pp. 712-19.

MAYS, J.B. (1954), *Growing Up in the City*, Liverpool: Liverpool University Press.

MEAD, G.H. (1934), *Mind, Self and Society*. Chicago: University of Chicago Press.

MEASOR, L. (1985), 'Interviewing in ethnographic research' in Burgess R.G. (ed.), *Qualitative Methodology and the Study of Education*, Lewes: Falmer Press.

MERTON, R.K. (1938), 'Social structure and Anomie', *American Sociological Review*, 3 (Oct) pp 672-682.

MERTON, R.K. (1957), *Social Theory and Social Structure*, New York: Free Press.

MILLER, W.B. (1958), 'Lower class culture as a generating milieu of gang delinquency', *Journal of Social Issues*, 14, pp. 5-19.

MILLER, W., MILLER, W.B., GEERTZ, H. and CUTTER, H. (1961), 'Aggression in a boys' street-corner gang', *Psychiatry*, 24, pp. 283-98.

MILLHAM, S., BULLOCK, R. and CHERRETT, P. (1972), 'Social control in organisations', *British Journal of Sociology*, 23, pp. 406-21.

MILLHAM, S., BULLOCK, R. and CHERRETT, P. (1975), *After Grace -Teeth*, London: HCB.

MILLHAM, S., BULLOCK, R. and CHERRETT, P. (1975b), 'A conceptual scheme for the comparative analysis of residential institutions' in Tizard, J., Sinclair, I. and Clarke, R.V.G. (eds.), *Varieties of Residential Experience*, London: Routledge & Kegan Paul.

MILLHAM, S., BULLOCK, R. and HOSIE, K. (1978), *Locking up Children*, Farnborough: Saxon House.

MORENO, J.L. (1953), *Who Shall Survive?*, New York: Beacon House.

MORRIS, A., GILLER, H., SZWED, E. and GEACH, H. (1980), *Justice for Children*, London: Macmillan.

MORRIS, P. and MORRIS, T. (1963), *A Sociological Study of an English Prison*, London: RKP.

++++

OSBORN, S.G. and WEST, D.J. (1978), 'The effectiveness of various predictions of criminal careers', *Journal of Adolescence*, 1, pp.101-117.

++++

PARKER, T. (1970), *The Frying Pan: A Prison and its Prisoners*, London: Hutchinson.

PARSONS, T., BALES, R.F. and SHILS, E.A. (1954), *Working Papers in the Theory of Action*, Glencoe: Free Press.

PATRICK, J. (1973), *A Glasgow Gang Observed*, London: Eyre-Methuen.

PHILLIPS, B. (1978), *Patterns of Juvenile Crime*, London: Peel Press.

PINCHBECK, I. and HEWITT, M. (1973), *Children in English Society*, London: Routledge & Kegan Paul.

POLSKY, H. (1962), *Cottage Six*, New York: Wiley.

PROBYN, W. (1977), *Angel Face: the Making of a Criminal*, London: Allen & Unwin.

++++

QUINNE, W.V.O. (1972), 'Some methodological reflections on current linguistic theory' in Harman G. and Davidson D. (eds.), *Semantics of Natural Language*. Reidel.

RADZINOWICZ, L. and KING, J. (1977), *The Growth of Crime: The International Experience*, London: Hamish Hamilton.

ROBERTS, K. (1974), 'The entry into employment: an approach towards a general theory' in Williams W.M. (ed.), *Occupational Choice: A Selection of Papers from the Sociological Review*, London: Allen and Unwin.

ROBINS, L. (1978), 'Sturdy childhood predictors of adult antisocial behaviour: replications from longitudinal studies', *Psychological Medicine*, 8, pp.611-622

ROOK, C. (1979), *The Hooligan Nights*, Oxford: OUP.

ROSE, G. (1956), 'The sociological analysis of borstal training', *British Journal of Delinquency*, VI, 3.

ROSE, G. (1956b), 'Sociometric analysis and observation in a borstal institution, *British Journal of Delinquency*, VI, 4.

ROSE, G. (1959), 'Status and grouping in a borstal institution', *British Journal of Delinquency*, ix, 258-273.

ROSE, G. (1962), 'Status grouping in a borstal' in Johnston N., Savitz L. and Wolfgang M.E. *The Sociology of Punishment and Correction*, New York: John Wiley.

RUGGLES-BRISE, E. (1921), *The English Prison System*, London: Macmillan.

RUTHERFORD, A. (1986), *Growing Out of Crime*, Harmondsworth: Penguin.

RUTTER, M. and GILLER, H. (1983), *Juvenile Delinquency: Trends and Perspectives*, Harmondsworth: Penguin.

++++

SAUSSURE, F. de. (1974), Course in General Linguistics: London: Fontana and Collins.

SCHMUCK, R. and LOHMAN, A. (1965), Peer Relations and Personality Development, Englewood-Cliffs: Prentice Hall.

SCHRAG, C. (1954), 'Leadership among prison inmates', American Sociological Review (Feb) 19: pp. 37-42.

SCOTT, P. (1964), 'Approved school success rates', British Journal of Criminology, IV, p. 525.

SCOTT, R. (1969), *The Making of Blind Men*, New York: Russell and Sage.

SHERIF, M. and SHERIF, C.W. (1964), *Reference Groups*, New York: Harper.

SHIBUTANI, T. (1955), 'Reference groups as perspectives', *American Journal of Sociology*, IX, pp. 562-9.

SHIBUTANI, T. (1966), *Improvised News: A Sociological Study of Rumour*, Indianapolis: Bobbs-Merrill Co.

SHUTZ, A. (1970), *Reflections on the Problem of Relevance*, Yale: OUP.

SILVERMAN, D. (1970), *The Theory of Organisations: A Sociological Perspective*, London: Heinemann.

SOLZHENITSYN, A. (1968), *One Day in the Life of Ivan Denisovich*, Harmondsworth: Penguin.

STENHOUSE, L. (1984), 'Library access, library use and user education in academic sixth forms: an autobiographical account' in Burgess, R.J. (ed.), *The Research Process in Educational Settings: Ten Case Studies*, Lewes: Falmer Press.

STEWART, A., PRENDY, K. and BLACKBURN, M. (1980), *Social Stratification and Occupations*, Oxford: MacMillan.

STEWART, G. and TUTT, N.S. (1987), *Children in Custody*, Aldershot: Avebury.

STRATTA, E. (1976), *The Education of Borstal Boys: A Study of their Educational Experiences prior to, and during, Borstal Training*, London: Routledge & Kegan Paul.

SUTHERLAND, E.H. and CRESSEY, D. (1970), *Principles of Criminology*, Philadelphia, Lippincott.

SYKES, G.M. (1958), *The Society of Captives*, Princeton: Princeton University Press.

++++

TAJFEL, H. (1978), 'Social Categorisation, Social Identity and Social Compassion', in Tajfel H. (ed.), *Differentiation between Social Groups*, New York: Academic Press.

THRASHER, F.M. (1927), *The Gang*, Chicago: University of Chicago Press.

TUTT, N.S. (1973), 'Achievement motivation and the criminal personality', *British Journal of Social and Clinical Psychology*, Sept.

TUTT, N.S. (1974), *Care or Custody: Community Homes and the Treatment of Delinquency*, London: Darton, Longman and Todd.

TUTT, N.S. (1976), 'Recommittals of Juvenile Offenders', *British Journal of Criminology*, XVI, pp385-388.

TUTT, N.S. (1983), 'Diversion - what is it?', in Northamptonshire County Council/Centre of Youth, Crime and Community, University of Lancaster, *Diversion - Corporate Action with Juveniles*, March 1984.

++++

WADSWORTH, M. (1979), *Roots of Delinquency: Infancy, Adolescence and Crime,* Oxford: Martin Robertson.

WALKER, N. (1982), 'Unscientific, unwise, unprofitable or unjust?', *British Journal of Criminology*, 22, pp. 276-284.

WEST, D.J. (1982), *Delinquency: its Roots, Careers and Prospects,* London: Heinemann.

WEST, D.J. and FARRINGTON, D.P. (1973), *Who Becomes Delinquent?*, London: Heinemann.

WEST, D.J. and FARRINGTON, D.P. (1977), *The Delinquent Way of Life,* London: Heinemann.

WHEELER, S. (1961), 'Socialization in correctional communities', *American Sociological Review*, 26, p. 697.

WHYTE, W.F. (1943), *Street Corner Society: the Social Organisation of a Chicago Slum,* Chicago: University of Chicago.

WHYTE, W.F. (1982), 'Interviewing in field research' in Burgess R.G. (ed.), *Field Research: a Sourcebook and Field Manual,* London: Allen & Unwin.

WILLIS, P. (1977), *Learning to Labour: How Working Class Kids Get Working Class Jobs,* Farnborough: Saxon House.

WINCH, P. (1958), *The Idea of a Social Science,* London: Allen Lane.

WITTGENSTEIN, L. (1958), *Philosophical Investigations,* Oxford: Blackwell.

WOODS, P. (1986), *Inside Schools: Ethnography in Educational Research,* London: Routledge & Kegan Paul.

++++

YABLONSKY, L. (1967), *The Violent Gang,* Harmondsworth: Penguin.

Index